OPENING DOORS
to a
RICHER ENGLISH CURRICULUM

for ages 6 to 9

BOB COX
with Leah Crawford and Verity Jones

Illustrations by Victoria Cox

Crown House Publishing Limited
www.crownhouse.co.uk

First published by

Crown House Publishing Ltd

Crown Buildings, Bancyfelin, Carmarthen, Wales, SA33 5ND, UK

www.crownhouse.co.uk

and

Crown House Publishing Company LLC

PO Box 2223, Williston, VT 05495, USA

www.crownhousepublishing.com

British Library Cataloguing-in-Publication Data

A catalogue entry for this book is available from the British Library.

Print ISBN 978-178583398-4

Mobi ISBN 978-178583460-8

ePub ISBN 978-178583461-5

ePDF ISBN 978-178583462-2

LCCN 2019945821

Printed and bound in the UK by

Gomer Press, Llandysul, Ceredigion

For Barbara and Tom,
with love

Foreword

I love this book and its companion volume. If I were still a teacher then it would become a key resource for planning, alongside earlier books in the 'Opening Doors' series.

Miroslav Holub's poem 'The Door' has always been one of my favourites (it is included in the 10 to 13 volume). I first stumbled across this little gem in an anthology called *Voices*, edited by Geoffrey Summerfield, when I was at school. For me, the poem represented an idea about possibility, having the courage to step through the door, come what may – seize the moment, be brave, be bold and see what happens. It has become a metaphor for my life in many ways. The 'Opening Doors' movement believes that as schools and teachers we should be opening doors of educational opportunity for children by placing great literature at the heart of the English curriculum – and by literature, I mean the whole range of quality writing from poetry to narrative and elegant non-fiction.

Along with Bob Cox, Leah Crawford and Verity Jones, I believe that we should be teaching English as a subject and selecting the texts that we study because of their lasting quality – because they provide challenge, are worth experiencing and broaden a child's reading and writing repertoire. I do not believe that choosing books or poems should be dominated by trying to find a text that matches a topic. That way, English is no longer a subject but the servant of other subjects, on the basis of no solid evidence that the approach improves learning in those subjects, let alone English.

A school that is mapping out an English programme will be thinking about placing the finest literature at the heart of the curriculum. Nothing else will do. The choice of texts needs careful consideration. If children are to enjoy and be able to make something of Walter de la Mare's 'The Listeners' in Year 6, then what progression of texts is needed to provide the stepping stones that gradually and cumulatively prepare children for such richness? How do we build the ability to access challenging literature with confidence so that children can comfortably appreciate, enjoy and, critically, read the very best that literature has to offer? If this is not well considered, and the stepping stones are not carefully mapped, children arrive in Year 6 and are ill-prepared for the demands of poets such Ted Hughes, Edward Thomas, Emily Dickinson, Philip Gross and William Blake. The same principle applies to their arrival in Year 7, with the Key Stage 3 curriculum being sequenced to build for Key Stage 4 work.

The 'Opening Doors' movement has been working with great texts and building a repertoire to draw upon when writing with children. The units of work map out possibilities for entering the world of the text, deepening understanding and engagement. The importance of reading aloud should not be underestimated. Children should experience how the language flows, responding to the meaning but also hearing and being moved by the musical tune of the text. It is worth mapping and chorally learning the poems. Key paragraphs or telling sentences could also be learned or performed orally, so that the close and careful study of the texts helps children to internalise the language patterns of great writing. Loitering with great literature, spending time rereading and discussing, and performing with expression allows the language to permeate and embed into children's linguistic competency, adding to their store of imaginative possibility and literary language patterns. Imagine putting the words of William Blake into a child's mind forever!

When Ted Hughes was at Cambridge, he used to get up at five o'clock every morning and read a Shakespeare play. His deep and rich reading put the language and imaginative world of a genius inside his mind. His reading grew his inner world. In the same way, great English teaching grows the imagination and language repertoire of every child through experiencing great literature in depth. If the reading curriculum is meagre, then children will never possess the world of great books and their writing will always be a thin echo of their low-level reading.

'Opening Doors' books are based on what works in classrooms. Over the years, I learned as a teacher that certain texts lend themselves to teaching. For instance, William Blake's 'The Tyger' has always worked well for me in terms of challenging interpretation and leading to deep discussion. Kit Wright's 'The Magic Box' has always stimulated great imaginative writing. Anthony Browne's *Voices in the Park* has never failed to yield up riches during oral comprehension. The units in *Opening Doors to a Richer English Curriculum* have been road-tested and refined in the light of teaching experience. I like the way the authors provide suggestions but expect that the teacher will bring their own ideas to deepen the experience for their children's needs. There is room for performance, drama, taster drafts, mini-writes, imitating lines, writing in response and, of course, deep oral comprehension, where children talk their way to an understanding with the teacher orchestrating the discussion.

Loitering with a worthwhile text that has layers of meaning helps children to move beyond having a passing acquaintance with a poem or story to a deeper relationship. Some children will need to read and reread a text so they can move beyond just being able to decode, shifting into the possibility of deeper understanding. Initial responses can be gathered and discussed, including aspects of what seems significant, interesting or worth discussing, as well as aspects that are mystifying. Spending time discussing vocabulary and the different shades of meaning that so many words and phrases hold is an important part of helping texts to yield up their riches.

What else does an English curriculum need? Across each year, novels, short stories, poetry, non-fiction and film should be identified to build the children's reading and writing stamina. These core books can then be drawn upon during specific units when working with focused texts. A rich reading programme will provide lines of reference and further reading to supplement each unit. Great books will also be useful to develop the children's writing skills: drawing on a range of examples, demonstrating writing techniques such as foreshadowing, and building atmosphere through setting, shift of viewpoint or tension. Such a reading programme provides the daily 'read aloud' sessions for each class and ideally should be supplemented with class sets of books (or at least enough for one between two) so that students can read along, pause, reread and draw upon passages for further work.

Drama can be used to slow the moment in a text, engage emotionally with thought and action, and deepen understanding. Drama also leads well into writing because the writing then arises from the imagined and enacted experience, which throws up more insight and possibility to draw upon when writing. The issue is selecting the right moment and the right activity rather than just deciding to do a bit of 'hot seating'. Where in a text would the reading be deepened through drama, and what strategy should be used? Most teachers have a small repertoire – hot seating, freeze-framing and conscience alley for decision-making – and that's about it! 'Opening Doors' books are full of techniques to extend your toolkit of strategies.

'Opening Doors' approaches also suggest that as teachers we should be writing for and with children to open up possibilities. When shifting into writing, some texts will lend themselves to very obvious imitation. A poem such as 'The Door' could be used as a straightforward model, so the children write an imitation using the same pattern. However, rich reading can also act as a springboard into other ideas and forms of writing. The books list possibilities, but I would also try making a list with the class to open up their ideas and encourage independent thinking.

A key aspect for anyone planning an English curriculum is the notion of developing and revisiting 'key concepts' to create a curriculum that is based on cumulative learning of the big, underlying ideas. This can be supplemented by thinking carefully about deep themes in texts that might be revisited. For instance, the children might experience the story of 'Beauty and the Beast' in Year 2: a tale of a character rejected by society who forms a relationship with someone who sees beyond any physical barrier. This theme may also be revisited in Year 4 through Michael Morpurgo's *Why the Whales Came* or in Year 8 when looking at *The Phantom of the Opera*.

The 'Opening Doors' books leave plenty of space for new texts, enthusiasm and experimentation because the underlying pattern for teaching is easily transferable. The process soon becomes embedded, and that makes teaching easier as our attention shifts from planning the sequence to being able to focus more on the children's learning.

All of this work has to be underpinned by a strong commitment to developing children as readers and writers. In an ideal world, every school would have a wonderfully equipped library so the children have a range of texts to choose from in their individual reading. To acquire fluency and confidence in reading, children may well want to storm their way through popular texts. However, teachers of English will want to grow each child as a reader, introducing them to new authors and styles, nudging them on to richer texts where the reading experience is not just a glib giggle but becomes something deeper and more long-lasting. Children will never really become great readers until they begin to tackle great texts and learn that sustaining their reading with a classic bears fruit. By the same token, they will never become great writers if their reading is thin gruel because their reading will be echoed in their writing.

The 'Opening Doors' teacher is also aware of their own reading and writing life, sharing their love of books with their classes and modelling being a reader. They also enjoy writing for and with their classes, sharing their own drafts as well as composing with the children. In this way, the 'Opening Doors' classroom becomes a community of readers and writers where the challenge of great literature and finely crafted writing, which focuses on the effect on the reader, becomes an everyday joy.

Pie Corbett

Contents

Acknowledgements

The 'Opening Doors' series of books has been developed thanks to feedback and encouragement from schools across the UK (and beyond), and their trialling of materials. It is much appreciated and, indeed, inspiring to hear from so many schools who are using the ideas.

In particular, we would like to thank staff and pupils from:

Alverstoke Junior School, Hampshire

Ash Grove Academy, Cheshire

Aston St Mary's C of E Primary, Hertfordshire

Breamore CE Primary School, Hampshire – with thanks to Emma Clark

The Brent Primary School, London

Briar Hill Primary School, Northamptonshire – with thanks to Ian Hickman

Cherbourg Primary, Hampshire

Chiltern Hills Academy, Buckinghamshire – with thanks to Sue Putnam

Coastlands Primary School, Pembrokeshire – with thanks to Wenda Davies

College Town Primary, Berkshire

Crofton Hammond Infants, Hampshire – with thanks to Jacky Halton

Crookham Junior School, Hampshire

Freegrounds Infants School, Hampshire

Gearies Primary School, Essex – with thanks to Bob Drew

Greenacres Primary Academy, Greater Manchester – with thanks to Tim Roach

Grove Primary School, Redbridge, London

Hale Primary School, Hampshire

Hillcrest Academy, West Yorkshire – with thanks to Sam Collier

Hordle Primary School, Hampshire

Kensington Prep School, Fulham, London

Malmesbury Park School, Dorset – with thanks to Nuala Price

Mottingham Primary School, Bromley, London

Overton Primary School, Hampshire

Poulner Infants School, Hampshire

Poulner Junior School, Hampshire

Red Barn Primary School, Hampshire

Ringwood Junior School, Hampshire

Robin Hood Junior School, Surrey

Rowner Junior School, Hampshire – with thanks to Emily Weaver

Southroyd Primary School, West Yorkshire – with thanks to Emma Kilsby

St Augustine's Catholic Primary School, Surrey

St Lawrence School and Chobham cluster, Surrey

St Mathew's, West Midlands – with thanks to Sonia Thompson

St Oswald's CE Primary School, North Yorkshire

Surbiton High Girls' Preparatory School, Kingston upon Thames, London

Tanglin Trust School, Singapore

Unicorn Trust Schools – with thanks to Sue Robertson

Westbourne Primary School, Surrey

Westbury Park Primary School, Bristol

Western Downland Primary School, Hampshire

Wicor Primary School, Hampshire

And also:

Ad Astra Academy Trust

Aspire Education Trust

Centre for Literacy in Primary Education

Hampshire Local Education Authority

Herts for Learning

High Performance Learning – with thanks to Deborah Eyre

Isle of Man, Department of Education and Children

Just Imagine Story Centre

Lancashire Local Education Authority

Leeds Local Education Authority

National Association for the Teaching of English – with thanks to Janet Gough

Optimus Education

Osiris Educational

Research Rich Pedagogies – with thanks to Professor Teresa Cremin and the United Kingdom Literacy Association/ Open University

Talk for Writing – with thanks to Pie Corbett

Write Time – with thanks to Victoria Bluck

Writing for Pleasure – with thanks to Ross Young and Felicity Ferguson

Above all, huge thanks to the team at Crown House Publishing, without whom the 'Opening Doors' series would never have been written!

Introduction

The 'Opening Doors' series has been supporting teachers' passion for quality texts since 2014. At home and abroad, the books have been signposting richer approaches to English in schools keen to exploit the learning opportunities afforded by a depth of challenge for all learners. We have had the pleasure of hearing from many teachers about their pupils' delight in discovering famous writers, their growing relish for learning about a variety of literary styles, and their increasing access to literature and cultural capital. Of course, this applies to all abilities and in some schools this has led to the word 'ability' being reviewed because 'Opening Doors' strategies work on fundamental principles through which *all* learners can be challenged. The highly ambitious approaches offer fresh goals and continual curiosity, but the scaffolds and interventions include and inspire everyone. Each step can represent new knowledge and learning gained in chunks as appropriate for each pupil.

It has been vital that the access strategies enable all pupils to discover just how quirky, fascinating and full of wonder great writing can be. There are big ideas in the extracts and poems we choose for 'Opening Doors', and this is important. The originality and beauty of the text leads the classroom discussion, whilst metaphors, adverbs and prepositional phrases, for example, are taught and modelled in context. Pupils are immersed in reading journeys via quality texts, whilst the dialogic talk, philosophy and teaching of new knowledge combine to create rich learning experiences.

As we have toured schools in the UK and abroad, evidence of the positive impact of challenging texts on pupils' work has grown – there are some examples on the Crown House Publishing website.[1] Have a browse and then make links with the first two books – you could even use the pupils' work as a resource in your lessons.

Teachers learn more themselves every time they explore a challenging new text, and there is a tendency to aim higher as a habit. Once we aspire to something almost out of reach, we might just get there! This goes for teachers and pupils: risk-taking becomes endemic and the acquisition of new vocabulary becomes a daily habit. Some of the new words are only half-grasped initially, but it still represents an important encounter for pupils. Children may have to meet vocabulary in various different contexts over time for the meaning to become fully assimilated. Our own adult relationships with new vocabulary may suggest a similar journey.

In this book, and in its companion for the 10 to 13 age group, we want to show how the use of quality texts is not a separate strand of the curriculum or special content for a project day. It can be an integral part of the whole curriculum, with continuity and progression built in. I (Bob) have been working with co-authors Leah Crawford and Verity Jones on both of these new books, which has been a real privilege. Together, we have provided fifteen units of work (thirty across both volumes) which will give you lots of ideas for building the metalanguage and new knowledge of texts needed to raise standards in the most exciting way possible.

---

[1] See https://www.crownhouse.co.uk/featured/opening-doors-to-famous-poetry-and-prose-pupils-work.

Opening Doors to a Richer English Curriculum will support your vision for English, but it will also offer the core principles and detailed units of work that will enable it to be realised. A curriculum with a combination of quality picture books, children's fiction and literature provides a much more appetising diet than is sometimes offered in schools. With effective transition to Key Stage 3, this will become a journey where reading for challenge starts to become the greatest pleasure any child can encounter – nurtured by sensitive and knowing teachers. We have always thought that what teachers do best is to make new learning possible for all. As Timothy Shanahan (2017) observes, 'start kids out with complex texts that they cannot read successfully; then teach them to read those texts well'.

We have included a great range of texts both as the core of each unit and as link reading. We have incorporated some contemporary texts to show how past and present co-exist and how various literary styles can be taught using similar principles, all of which are open to further adaptation. Non-fiction gets a mention too, as many schools have started to apply the key principles for depth to all text types. For the first time, we have also suggested key concepts around which the curriculum can be built, with the units providing examples with which you can work. Developing concepts through which English can be taught will offer you the chance to plan a rich map of learning – one that the whole school will understand. One of the things we have enjoyed most about the 'Opening Doors' series is seeing teachers grow in confidence as the books signpost the way to their own innovations.

We are very much in favour of the 'continuing' part of continuing professional development (CPD), and we want to support teachers' growth and their love of learning. Growing a richer English curriculum will enable the most natural, reflective and evaluative CPD to take place in your classroom every single day. The extra challenges afforded by richer texts will stimulate your own learning far more than standard texts. As teachers, we have to think harder, set more profound questions, play with vocabulary and teach specific concepts – but we get so much more back from our pupils, and there are no dull routines!

Summary of the key principles

As befits a brief introduction, we can only list here the major principles and strategies that have emerged from our work in schools. This is not a model for teaching English, but it is a framework to use as part of your own curriculum design – shaped by you and fit for purpose in your school and with your children. See the framework example on pages 6–7.

Access strategies and 'beyond the limit' link reading

We call this series of books 'Opening Doors' because access is fundamental to new learning. Without the teaching strategies to unlock learning potential, it is likely that new language, genres and styles could be intimidating. But teachers release a whole world of possibility by demonstrating how meaning can be grasped and new literary satisfactions experienced. That's the joy of challenge!

In this book there are a range of access strategies: pictures, questions, links to existing knowledge/experience and slivers of text (adapting the length of the material is far better than excluding anyone from the shared excitement). Each unit has a suggestion for a key strategy with a snappy title. This is designed to support the teaching of comprehension because it enables pupils to start learning about different ways to understand a text.

Of course, it is the link reading that will boost children's comprehension the most. We have worked with schools on linking a range of texts to the core objective and planning for whole-text reading as an expected part of the curriculum. Every term and every year, the objectives and texts get progressively harder, but always within the context of a broad choice. Whereas the term 'wider reading' has often been used, we prefer 'link reading' because it is planned into the curriculum for everyone (see pages 6–7 for an example of the big picture of the objectives and link reading). We also call this the 'beyond the limit' section to emphasise that it is the depth of quality reading expected by schools, linked with reading for pleasure acquired more independently, that will support accelerated progress.

Framework Planning Example

Unit 6: Faceless

'Prince Kano' by Edward Lowbury

Opening Doors key strategy: only connect!

Objectives which prompt deeper learning journeys:

❦ Can you understand how poets use associations in readers' minds?

❦ Can you include common associations in the images you invent in your own poem?

❦ Can you make these associations original?

Teach *functional English* as appropriate in this deeper context.

Develop a deeper understanding of connections and associations via link reading:

- 'The Watchers' by Joseph Coelho
- 'The Statue' by James Reeves
- 'Sea-Rock' by Grace Nichols
- 'The Sea' by James Reeves
- 'The Forlorn Sea' by Stevie Smith
- 'How to Cut a Pomegranate' by Imtiaz Dharker

Quality text to quality writing journeys:

Apply what you have learnt from Edward Lowbury to write a poem developing your own use of connections with the reader:

- Princess Katrine
- The White Hooded Rider
- Invisible Women
- The Raven and the Wood
- The Round Table
- The Walking Stick and the Child

In *Understanding Reading Comprehension* (2015: 51), Wayne Tennent argues that 'when children come to the reading of written text they are not blank canvasses. They bring both life and linguistic knowledge to each reading experience.' Schools that are building link reading and simultaneously facilitating reading for pleasure are deepening the knowledge that can be applied to the next challenge.

Taster drafts

The idea of a taster draft is for pupils to write early on in the process to help promote their engagement with, and understanding of, the text. The task is usually time limited and/or word limited. Pupils love the freedom this allows, and teachers love the chance to teach spelling, punctuation and grammar, as well as aspects of style, through the resulting mini-plenaries.

Not only is much of this early learning embedded for the long term, but pupils are also eager to hear the full text. We rarely read out the entire text to the children at the start of the activity, but after attempting their own writing they often beg to hear the famous writer's work. You can hear a pin drop as they listen to the reading. It's no surprise that further questions follow.

Reading journeys

When we mention the word 'comprehension' to pupils in schools, we nearly always get a response which is at best neutral and at worst a shrug or scornful look of boredom. A few times pupils have even said that it is what happens at 2pm every Tuesday! Often there is a link between comprehension and being tested. This doesn't have to be the case. Rather than being something done to you, it can be much more exciting – a reading journey or a dialogue about half-grasped vocabulary or the way a narrative has been expressed. Predictions, questions, new knowledge on technique and effect, and the sharing of ideas can all be part of a reading journey.

You may have your own term, but why not drop the word 'comprehension' if it elicits groans or negativity? In 'Opening Doors' books, we use a big 'Opening Doors' question, with support interventions deployed as appropriate to build skills and knowledge. The glossary also provides prompts for helpful terms and theories. Remember: in your classroom, decisions about the use of resources, questions and strategies pave the way to deeper comprehension for your pupils, so always think of yourself as a pioneer in opening up quality reading routes.

Support questions

Each unit includes an ambitious set of questions, not as a test but to provide a basis for teaching and learning dialogues. The questions are aspirational – a goal for mastery – because all pupils are on a learning journey. Support scaffolds are suggested for those pupils who are struggling, and there are greater depth questions for those who are ready for them. Some pupils will be able to answer the main 'Opening Doors' question without much support, and even move on to the greater depth question if you are happy that their answer is thorough. Advanced pupils should not waste time on anything too easy.

Differentiation occurs through the learning stage, not separate content or objectives.

The radial layouts have proved popular as a tool through which differentiated interventions can be made appropriately for each pupil. Flexibility is vital, so it can be advantageous to create guided groups, according to need, so pupils can learn to the best of their ability at each stage. Some pupils may surprise you in being ready for harder work, whilst other pupils may need more advice and scaffolding. However, greater depth opportunities are always built into expectations.

Excellent responses will (include)

You will find success criteria lists throughout the book, but please don't use them as an arid or discrete list. They are designed to enable teachers to explore just how deep they can go using literary texts. More challenging poems, for example, may need a lot of rereading – but the love of a poem can grow through familiarity. It is possible to prioritise one or two criteria and convert them into child-friendly language. In this way, teaching teams can have rich conversations of their own about language and its effect, about themes and about the appeal of the writing.

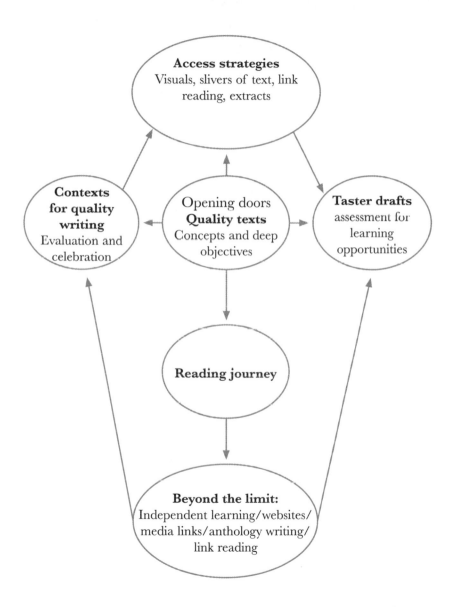

Access strategies
Visuals, slivers of text, link reading, extracts

Contexts for quality writing
Evaluation and celebration

Opening doors
Quality texts
Concepts and deep objectives

Taster drafts
assessment for learning opportunities

Reading journey

Beyond the limit:
Independent learning/websites/ media links/anthology writing/ link reading

Key concepts

Mapping key concepts at Key Stages 1, 2 and 3 will facilitate a genuine curriculum journey, with revisiting built in via texts which get progressively harder. Remember that you are teaching English, not 'doing' a text. *Opening Doors to a Richer English Curriculum* will signpost your deeper thinking on a map of learning for English. The diagram on page 11 provides a framework for the many ways in which quality writing can be achieved using 'Opening Doors' strategies.

Deep objectives

Having established multilayered concepts for each unit, we have once again suggested using objectives which can go much deeper and through which the concepts can be taught. We have used open-ended questions for these objectives throughout the book because pupils seem to find goals set in question form motivating. Aim to teach aspects of English as part of a richer journey to learning – for example, you can plan for functional English or a targeted aspect of English (like noun phrases) as part of that bigger goal. In this way, spelling, punctuation and grammar can be contextualised much more successfully.

Occasionally, it may be useful to teach pupils about a common misconception. But when lessons focus on one specific aspect of English, especially when this becomes a habit, the curriculum can be narrowed to what we call a 'letter box' approach, with the same few discrete aspects of English delivered and tested again and again. This is the opposite of a curriculum that is deep, rich and full of curiosity.

Wings to fly

Wings to fly are suggested titles with options built in. The phrase actually comes from an evaluation we once heard: that a teacher's pupils had been given 'wings to fly, not drills to kill'. The idea is to learn from a great writer and then apply this creatively to make quality texts link with quality writing.

The 'Opening Doors' team is continually collecting feedback from schools. The acknowledgement list includes just a few of the schools to whom we are grateful for their astute thinking and astonishing work, improving both their pupils' comprehension and writing skills. From this feedback has come a perception that teachers are beginning to use a greater range of literary texts in their curriculum planning, and we certainly hope that we have helped.

I (Bob) call this going 'Beyond the Highwayman', after the famous Alfred Noyes poem which has become a favourite in many primary classrooms. I realised during an INSET I was running that teachers were wary of the difficulties that a new literary text might pose. But when I talked to them about 'The Highwayman', 'The Lady of Shalott' or 'The Listeners' (all poems with challenging and fascinating styles and themes), it emerged that it was more an issue of unfamiliarity when it came to new texts. The complexity of the text was not the problem; there was just the need to get acquainted with it. So, I hope

Opening Doors to a Richer English Curriculum for Ages 6 to 9 will help you all to go 'Beyond the Highwayman'.

Resources

As we have written the series, the following books and organisations have provided particular inspiration and often echoes of the challenge ethos that we all hope to encourage:

Clements, James (2018). *Teaching English by the Book*. Abingdon: Routledge.

Eyre, Deborah (2016). *High Performance Learning: How to Become a World Class School*. Abingdon: Routledge.

Lemov, Doug, Driggs, Colleen and Woolway, Erica (2016). *Reading Reconsidered: A Practical Guide to Rigorous Literacy Instruction*. San Francisco, CA: Jossey-Bass.

Myatt, Mary (2018). *The Curriculum: Gallimaufry to Coherence*. Woodbridge: John Catt Educational.

Roche, Mary (2014). *Developing Children's Critical Thinking Through Picturebooks*. Abingdon: Routledge.

Tennent, Wayne, Reedy, David, Hobsbaum, Angela and Gamble, Nikki (2016). *Guiding Readers – Layers of Meaning: A Handbook for Teaching Reading Comprehension to 7–11 Year Olds*. London: University College London Institute of Education Press.

Centre for Literacy in Primary Education

Just Imagine Story Centre

Let's Think: Cognitive Acceleration

Research Rich Pedagogies – United Kingdom Literacy Association/Open University

Talk for Writing (Pie Corbett)

Part 1

Opening Doors
to Poetry

I Pulled a Hummingbird Out of the Sky

'Wind' by Dionne Brand

Opening Doors key strategy: first-person power

Can you understand how the wind could seem like a person in a poem?

Can you write powerfully about a raging wind?

Dionne Brand captures the moods of a Caribbean wind with subtlety and power in this poem, showing a huge imaginative scope of ideas. We love the beauty expressed in carrying a song or lifting up a wave – and every word counts, especially the verbs. Point out the difference between 'made', so full of certainty and threat, with 'hurried a stream', which is more persuasive and harrying. If your pupils can understand the deft precision of the descriptions, then they will also start to appreciate the impact of the first-person narrative and learn much about the craft of poetry.

There are useful cross-references with the **personification** work in Units 4 and 9, though this time your pupils can focus on the intensity of a first-person poem, with every line commencing with the voice of the wind.

Access strategies

Try a **bookends approach**. Offer the first four lines and the last three. It gives a tantalising glimpse into the personality of the wind:

I pulled a hummingbird out of the sky one day
 but let it go,
I heard a song and carried it with me
 on my cotton streamers, …
I became a breeze, bored and tired,
and hovered and hung and rustled and lay
 where I could.

Resource 2

Encourage the children to focus on the song. This is a particularly original feature: the wind is personified as hearing birdsong! Remember, this is no hurricane or gale. There is subtlety in this, so the poetic opportunities are greater. The song is then carried on cotton streamers. What might this mean?

Ask the children for some brief **taster drafts**. This could be around the concept of hearing sounds. How can the wind 'hear' anything? Ask them to imagine a wind blowing across their home or school. Which sounds are collected, passed on or transformed? Keep the taster draft word or time limited. It's short burst writing with a keen purpose.

Bob says ...

Ask for imitation to help the children trial, invent and experiment with ideas. Taster drafts have proved very successful in schools because they give teachers the opportunity to offer advice according to need. It sets the writing process in action just when the pupils are getting curious - not when it is almost the end of the day and the momentum has died.

Here are some taster drafts from pupils at Red Barn Primary School in Hampshire, where some impressive initiatives have been led by an inspiring teacher, Gemma Loveless.

I dropped it in a dark, luminous forest,

And heard the threatening screams of the flowers waking in horror.

Rhiannon Thomson

I dropped it in an abandoned dark desert where there was no life – no soul – no nothing to be seen.

Saya Forghani

I lifted a song from the crashing waves of the sunlit beach,

But let it go,

I dropped it in the magical woodlands and listened intently to the bluebells chiming with joy.

Lailah Castro-Garrick

I dropped into the clear blue ocean and listened to the heart of the sea sing beautifully and I heard tears of joy around the world.

Grace Nunez

Now get the children thinking about the ending:

- How can a breeze be tired?
- What is the effect of four verbs together, separated by 'and'?
- How do the meanings of the verbs differ?

Give your pupils the next three verbs which start lines and ask them to write what the wind did:

- 'I dropped …'
- 'I made … '
- 'I pushed … '

After taking feedback from the pupils, ask them to invent their own verbs for the changing power of the wind and write some new lines The best lines could be displayed or recited. Now, the children are primed to be fascinated by the setting and originality of the full poem!

Reading journeys

Wind

I pulled a hummingbird out of the sky one day
 but let it go,
I heard a song and carried it with me
 on my cotton streamers,
I dropped it on an ocean and lifted up a wave
 with my bare hands,
I made a whole canefield tremble and bend
 as I ran by,
I pushed a soft cloud from here to there,
I hurried a stream along a pebbled path,
I scooped up a yard of dirt and hurled it in the air,
I lifted a straw hat and sent it flying,
I broke a limb from a guava tree,
I became a breeze, bored and tired,
and hovered and hung and rustled and lay
 where I could.

Alternatively, you could cut the poem into strips and task the pupils with **sequencing** the lines in the correct order. This will synthesise what they have already learnt with a new opportunity to understand the decline in the wind's power throughout the poem.

Can your pupils devise symbols for each of the lines and illustrate the journey of the wind? This could be from the sky at the top of the poem to a tired breeze at the bottom. This activity should support an understanding of the big picture of the changing wind.

Now, ask the pupils which is their favourite line and why. Try a **continuum line** to show the verb meanings as they vary in force from strongest to weakest. This will teach them a lot about word meanings and precision.

Strong ⟵----------------------------------⟶ **Weak**

Pulled   Lay

This is very challenging but well worth doing. There will be debate even in the staffroom! How can we compare 'heard' with 'dropped'? Isn't 'pushed' stronger than 'hurried'? Ask the pupils to give reasons for their choices; it will help enormously with the quality of their writing later on.

Like many other suggestions for thinking in the 'Opening Doors' series, this is a metacognitive strategy which is designed to get the children thinking about learning and how learning takes place. The discussion arising from the continuum line will stretch the children's learning muscles (Claxton, 2005). Shirley Clarke, known internationally for her work on assessment for learning, said in a tweet: 'Metacognitive strategies work best when linked with learning contexts, rather than separated. So a lesson on what resilience means is not as effective as discussing resilience in the context of a challenging task for instance' (@shirleyclarke, 3 May 2018).

Music moments may also help to enhance the children's understanding of the poem: Chopin's 'Winter Wind' étude would complement the reading. The children could also explore the differences between van Gogh's 'Wheatfield with Crows' and Dionne Brand's depiction of a Caribbean wind. The painting can be found at: http://www.ibiblio.org/wm/paint/auth/gogh/fields/gogh.threatening-skies.jpg.

Bob says ...

Use the exercises in 'Opening Doors' to build resilience through debate about and exploration of challenging literature; learning how to learn is then contextual and relevant and not limited to discrete word games or quizzes.

Some more background on the Caribbean may enhance the children's understanding. Find visuals and information on the internet to explain:

- Canefields
- Guava tree
- Cotton
- Hummingbirds
- The climate and culture of the West Indies

You could now introduce **link reading** (from the list on pages 26–27) to build the pupils' knowledge. *Poetry Jump-Up*, edited by Grace Nichols, is a must – there are so many styles to appreciate and a range of poets from the Caribbean.

How many of your pupils can now begin to answer the **hardest question first**? It revolves around the **key concept** of using first-person power. Layer in support questions for those who need them and, as always, ensure you have planned opportunities for greater depth as part of the overall journey.

To keep the challenge high, make sure your curriculum content gives ample opportunity for the pupils to achieve the ambitious success criteria. You will need to explain some new knowledge, so the points on page 26 will help your teaching teams to be aware of what needs to be taught explicitly. Excellence success criteria can help you to pitch to the top from the start and to elicit some very special answers.

Support:
Collect all the different metaphors used through the verbs. Pick three to write about in detail.

Support:
Rewrite the first few lines in the third person. How is it different? What effect does each line beginning with 'I' have on the reader?

Support:
Why is the last line longer, and why does it have a different rhythm?

Can you write about the ways in which the poet gives the wind a voice and a personality?

Support:
How does the punctuation support the wind's 'voice'? Why is there no full stop until the end?

Support:
Understand more by reciting the poem. Can you learn it? Can you alter your expression to suit the dying wind?

Greater depth:
Compare your favourite images of the power of the wind with three other images from different poems. How do poets write 'wind' poems in distinctive ways?

Excellent responses will:

Key concept: use of first person

❧ Show how the wind as the first-person narrator gives a sense of power and control.

❧ Show a creative appreciation of the personality of the wind and reveal an understanding of the subtlety of the meaning and word usage.

Key concept: personification

❧ Demonstrate the ability to use examples and discuss word use.

❧ Explain some of the effects of personification, like the stream being 'hurried' and how it being in a rush helps us to visualise the water overflowing.

Beyond the limit – link reading

❧ 'Lines Composed in a Wood on a Windy Day' by Anne Brontë

❧ 'The Hail Storm in June, 1831' by John Clare

❧ 'Wind' by Joseph Coelho

❧ 'Once the Wind' by Shake Keane

❧ 'The Wind' by James Reeves

❧ 'The Wind' by Christina Rossetti

❧ *The Wind* by Walter de la Mare

- *The Wind Blew* by Pat Hutchins
- *Flood* by Alvaro F. Villa
- *Hurricane* by David Wiesner
- *A Caribbean Dozen* edited by John Agard and Grace Nichols

Bob says ...

Try to use these poems and stories in ways which support new learning and encourage links and evaluation as a habit: browsing and commenting, reading favourites, using ideas for the greater depth question, illustrating and image collecting. Offer reading time in class and ensure the link reading is ready on the desk in front of the pupils.

Wings to fly

Reading Dionne Brand's poem has meant learning about first-person power and personification, so ask the children to apply this to the titles that appeal to them most.

- How powerfully can you write about a raging wind?
  - I Pulled a Skylark Out of the Sky
  - I Had Ideas for the Straw Hat!
  - I Came in the Night
  - Wind Over the Water
  - Canefield and Cornfield
  - My Sounds

❧ From a Breeze to a Storm: My Journey

For inspiration, share these beautifully crafted poems by pupils from Red Barn Primary School:

Wind is Awoken

I have awoken from my deep slumber,
On a distant island,
I flattened trees,
And softened soil
And left a bear cub hanging from a branch,
I pushed the water to clean up my dirty work.
I carried aloft on the winds and the breeze,
Arousing to rapture the earth and the seas.

I capsized a small boat,
I created strong currents,
To waves settling on the seashore,

I came to a park,
I gently brushed the flowers and trees,
I then pushed a sailboat to help it on its journey.

I accidentally tumbled into a soft cloud.

I became a breeze, bored and tired, and hovered and hung, and rustled and lay where I could.

Archie Nelson

I Came in the Night

I came in the night,

Luminous black,

Dashing, darting,

I made the street lamps flicker and jerk as I swept by,

I saw the foxes and owls capture their prey,

I stole the last of the voices; I threw them into the sea,

I grasped the clocks' midnight chimes and muted the awakening sound,

And then the sun,

The burning rays,

The blinding light,

I fled to the misty shadows and disappeared.

Faith Gorman

My Dull Day

I awoke from my slumber to a dull day;

On one dull day something bothered me,

I wanted to strike and go on a rampage on one dull day,

On one dull day I travelled to the thunderous city,

I made everything lifeless around me,

I made a single train convulse and shattered the frosty windows as I strolled by,

I made the ocean do as I wished with one flick of the wrist,

I made that ocean vault over the city and watched it intently as it started to decay,

The more I weaken,

The more I grow,

The more I grow,

The more power I gain,

But for some reason I stopped and I started to perish, it was like me and my body had come to its end.

Callum Thatcher-Smith

The Wind Wants Revenge

I was dreaming about destruction,

When suddenly my soul was awakened and my spirit started soaring with revenge.

I heard a song from the tree tops and I carried it with me for my journey;

I made a whole city quiver as I banished my inner thoughts with an almighty gust of fury!

As I trampled the desert island, the trees bow down their heads and plead with me not to obliterate them like I did to many others.

Erin Wilkinson

The Woodpecker's Song

I was dreaming about a song,
My soul has awakened ... I heard it ...
My soul is soaring with happiness.

I looked down at the fields but
The fields were quivering with joy
By the woodpecker singing its heart out.

The echo is swishing from here to there ...
I pulled it from below; I dropped it
Onto a small island in the middle of the deep, blue
Ocean.
I pushed it from sea to land.

Caitlin Haswell

The reading should encourage originality, but if any of your pupils are stuck they could start with the list of verbs from the start of each line and create a different image using each one. They should try to craft very specific images which leave an impression – for example, we loved the idea of the trembling canefield.

For further challenge, think of four or five objects, settings or people that might be affected by the arrival of the wind and which might lead to some unique writing. Set the most interesting ideas you can come up with. You (or the pupils) could even create an anthology on the arrival and departure of the wind.

The link reading will enable your young writers to adapt ideas and create new ones. Consider how Joseph Coelho uses a fresh angle to portray the wind as blowing away the past in 'Wind' (from *Overheard in a Tower Block*).

I clamp my eyes against the wind
 and lean into its blast.
It sucks my clothes against my skin
 and blows away my past.

There are no limits to creativity in English!

What can your pupils come up with?

Unit 2

Do You Have Time to Stand and Stare?

'Leisure' by W. H. Davies

Opening Doors key strategy: repeat and create

Can you understand how repetition is used to good effect in poetry?

How well can you write your own poem using repetition and rhyming couplets?

Access strategies

'Leisure' is one of those poems that has endured changes in taste and trends in poetry to maintain its popularity. The theme of the need to reflect and empty the mind is as relevant today as ever and as important for young and old. It is a good poem for teaching about repetition and rhyme because it lends itself well to recitation and memorisation, for all the best reasons. The more the words are spoken, the more we appreciate the ideas behind them.

If we are serious about finding a balance in life and improving well-being, then poetry has a place. The theme of leisure is universal: we should not get so immersed in poetic techniques that we forget that the writing style has been chosen to communicate the meaning.

We can start by exploring some complexities of comprehension and vocabulary before we read the full poem. Let's take the first two lines:

What is this life if, full of care,

We have no time to stand and stare.

Using a **continuum line**, note down all the things your pupils can think of which might involve standing and staring. List everyday things at one end and very special events at the other. You might have to explain that 'stare' is not rude in this context – it means longer term reflection.

Everyday ←----------------------------------→ **Unusual**

Listening to a reading in assembly

Sunset on holiday

Sporting occasion

Now organise the children into groups and ask them to debate where on the continuum line the image of standing and staring should go.

This should support a whole-class discussion on the value of reflecting, digesting, watching, listening, admiring and thinking.

The other word which needs to be explored is 'care'. Ask the pupils to list as many definitions of care as they can. This will teach them how fascinating simple words can be and that writers are in the business of using the right word in the right place!

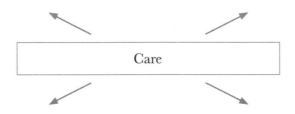

If you research the etymology (the study of word origins and how meanings have changed) of a word, you can extend your pupils' discoveries and encourage them to treat all vocabulary with the fascination of history. It will also improve their spelling as they begin to understand more about the ways in which words and meanings have evolved. This website will take you on some terrific journeys: www.etymonline.com.

Showing pupils how interesting a simple word can be is a good starting point – for example, you can establish that the backdrop of W. H. Davies' poem is anxiety. In *Closing the Vocabulary Gap* (2018: 71), Alex Quigley rightly emphasises the importance of word depth: 'When it comes to vocabulary knowledge and school success, "word depth" is probably more important than the breadth of our vocabulary.'

There are many opportunities in all the 'Opening Doors' books to explore vocabulary in rich ways, finding ambiguity, varied definitions and subtle nuances of meaning. For example, in Unit 4 in *Opening Doors to Quality Writing for Ages 6 to 9*, Christina Rossetti's 'What is Pink?' is used to stimulate colour imagery in poetry, focusing on white, black and red. You can now show your pupils the illustration and ask if they can find links in the image which give a hint as to the overall theme. Can they give it a suitable title?

Reading journeys

You could explore the image-making technique further by offering this line:

No time to see, in broad daylight,
Streams full of stars, like skies at night.

Ask the children for **taster drafts** using the same first line but with an imaginative second line. Go deeper with the comprehension before they begin writing:

❧ How can a stream be full of stars?

❧ What is a metaphor?

❧ What is a simile?

Maintaining the beauty of the image is key to creative discussions. There is a big jump from identifying figures of speech to understanding their context in a poem. This can be done via dialogic explorations and **didactic teaching**, but pertinent questions can help too:

❦ Have you ever stood and watched a stream flow?

❦ What might you see which could be like stars?

Some pupils may have never seen a stream, of course, so further resources may be needed.

When the children invent their own images, there is no reason to restrict them to a rural scene. The idea is for them to produce any image which implies peace and time to reflect – it could be anywhere. If you are teaching younger pupils, you may find it particularly useful to introduce images and word depth exploration stage by stage alongside more careful teaching. Their appreciation and feeling of comfort with the words needs time to grow.

W. H. Davies was a Welsh poet with an extraordinary life, and it is doubtful how much time he ever got to stand and stare. He spent much of his early life as a wandering traveller (some would say a tramp), traversing the Atlantic many times, losing his leg in an accident and being always on the verge of destitution. Eventually, his work came to the attention of major writers like George Bernard Shaw and D. H. Lawrence, and publishers started to become more interested. His most famous prose work is *The Autobiography of a Super-Tramp*, but he has also written many striking poems, which are often linked with the Georgian poetry movement. These poets favoured rural themes, reflection and poetry which could be understood and memorised. There are some examples in the **link reading** list which could be made available to pupils at the **reading journey** stage.

The key strategy in this unit is 'repeat and create', so you could make the link with your pupils that repetition is a creative tool for a poet and needs to be used to good effect. The link reading will give you more opportunities to teach about the ways in which repetition is used by writers and how your pupils might experiment with repetitions in their own writing.

A reading of the full poem now will have far more impact as the thinking, asking, predicting and writing has already boosted learning and increased anticipation.

Leisure

What is this life if, full of care,
We have no time to stand and stare.
No time to stand beneath the boughs,
And stare as long as sheep and cows.
No time to see, when woods we pass,
Where squirrels hide their nuts in grass.
No time to see, in broad daylight,
Streams full of stars, like skies at night.
No time to turn at Beauty's glance,
And watch her feet, how they can dance.
No time to wait till her mouth can
Enrich that smile her eyes began.
A poor life this if, full of care,
We have no time to stand and stare.

Support:

List all the things we have 'no time for'. Which is your favourite image?

Support:

Why are the first and final stanzas different?

How are the 'no time' stems different? Why?

Why do you think W. H. Davies used repetition so much in 'Leisure'?

Support:

Draw an image for each stanza. Perhaps draw the pictures around a circle as the poem ends back at the beginning.

Greater depth:

Why does W. H. Davies repeat the first stanza at the end but with 'a poor life this' as a new beginning?

Which poems from your link reading selection 'repeat and create' best?

Excellent responses will:

Key concept: use of repetition

❦ Explain how there are different verbs linked with 'no time' which introduce different images.

❦ Describe how the first and final stanzas provide a structure within which the repetitions produce a mounting rhythm.

Key concept: image-making

❦ Explain what each image means. For example, if Beauty is a dancer, how does the poet link watching a human with nature?

❦ Appreciate the exact effect of the images and how figures of speech can support imaginative writing.

Bob says ...

Introduce 'Leisure' to your colleagues. How many of them remember it from their own schooldays? Can your pupils learn to recite it by heart for an assembly? Memorising the poem will teach them a lot about the link between repetition and communicating meaning, and help them to capture the right pace. You can't rush this one and the last two lines must linger. Use the poem as a stimulus to collect favourite poems from the school community. How many have memorable repetitions? It is the music of poetry that helps to embed meaning into our hearts and minds.

Beyond the limit – link reading

Repetitions

- 'When Questions are Bliss' by John Agard
- 'Tall Tales' by Valerie Bloom
- 'I Adore Year 3' and 'The Look' by Carol Ann Duffy
- 'Empty Places' by Brian Moses
- 'Slowly' by James Reeves (Unit 3 in *Opening Doors to Quality Writing for Ages 6 to 9*)
- 'Busy Day' by Michael Rosen
- 'Anancy' by Andrew Salkey

Georgian poets (approximately 1910–1930)

- Rupert Brooke
- W. H. Davies
- Walter de la Mare (Unit 12 in *Opening Doors to Quality Writing for Ages 10 to 13*)
- Robert Graves
- A. E. Housman
- John Masefield

❦ Harold Monro (Unit 2 in *Opening Doors to Famous Poetry and Prose* and Unit 5 in *Opening Doors to Quality Writing for Ages 6 to 9*)

❦ Victoria (Vita) Sackville-West

❦ *Georgian Poetry*, edited by James Reeves

Wings to fly

Before developing the taster drafts, it may be helpful to make some specific teaching points about repetition. It is one of the most commonly used devices in poetry to create rhythm and express meaning, humour or profound ideas, but children can overuse it if they don't see enough examples. The link reading list is just a starting point, so do add your own favourites too.

Some repetitions are used sparingly; others dominate a poem. Sometimes, the pitch of a reading can rise as repetitions cluster; at other times, a repetition can introduce a new section of thought or an ending to link with a beginning.

The children's poetry writing on any of the suggested ideas that follow will be more successful if you have explored some of the many ways in which repetition can support the overall creative theme of a poem – repeat and create!

❦ Write your own poem using the first and last stanzas from 'Leisure' and the 'no time' stems for each verse, but create new images for reflection.

❦ Invent four new images of things we should all be noticing more and use each one in a stanza about leisure.

❦ More Time to …

❦ Write a poem about what we should notice more in one of these areas:

- ❧ A maths lesson
- ❧ Our own living room
- ❧ At night
- ❧ About ourselves
- ❧ On a car journey
- ❧ Assembly
- ❧ Towns or cities

❦ Write a funny poem using repetition about a day which is too busy. You will find Michael Rosen's 'Busy Day' very inspiring!

I (Bob) have tried composing a little piece where the impact of the poem has an unexpected effect on a boy's imagination. I hope you enjoy it. Why not have a go yourself?

Standing and Staring

(inspired by W. H. Davies)

Freddie stared out of his bedroom window.

The road outside was a cul-de-sac. Very little took place. He had some words rolling round in his head. That happened sometimes. A hubbub of words was trapped somewhere just inside his right ear. He wanted it to go away. Sometimes it happened at night.

So, he tried talking them out.

What is this life if, full of care,
We have no time to stand and stare.

Freddie thought staring was rude but Mrs Goodenough had
told them all that it wasn't that kind of staring the poet was
writing about. So, what was it about? She said try looking
around you, spend longer thinking, notice the passing of time.

Freddie looked at his watch. Five minutes had gone by and this
wasn't working and he admitted the words were still circling
through his brain in a huge logjam of confusion.

What is this life if, full of care,
We have no time to stand and stare.

Freddie looked closer, thought harder, stared for longer and the
world in his silent room and empty house began to change.

Opposite, a white blind opened and there was a face in the slit.
Two eyes stared. A long fingernail pointed outwards. Who was
she? Her hair had a yellow streak.

A bald man crossed the road with a Jack Russell. Freddie
noticed his brow knitting like a creased shirt. He had little legs
like the Jack Russell and the same rushed motion. Where was
he going?

A huge shape angled past the many parked cars. It was a
delivery van. Two people got out. Their jackets were like yellow
beacons. One was a very thin man with a beaky nose. The

other was a short woman with round glasses. She seemed to be telling the man what to do. Freddie saw them take tray after tray into the large detached house two along the way. She held up a piece of paper to the owner who had opened the door. Freddie heard them talking.

The owner's mouth opened large like a gawping goldfish. He raised his finger.

The thin man's beak was dropping, but the lady's head moved upwards. Then the owner got his phone out. Freddie saw them locked like people turned to stone.

The head was held, still and straight in the air, and the fingernail opposite was still on a slow, slow scratch across the blind. Freddie could hear it in one of his brain caves. The Jack Russell stopped his scurry and the creased-up man smiled like someone who knows something.

Freddie stared at the freeze-frame. It was full of stories, and yet it was nothing.

Above the street, regular puffy clouds had turned into a new kind of music in his head: a symphony of white sound, growing to a crescendo; bubble shapes across a blue sky; wafers and pearls chasing in concert; a darker patch swallowing the light on the van.

Freddie started. The blind opposite was pulled up. The painted nails scored the window. A round face looked sad.

She was looking at him!

Freddie realised he was in someone else's freeze-frame! More phrases found channels in his brain and he reached for his homework book.

'What is this life if, full of fear,

We have no time to see and hear.'

He had begun to write; the hubbub settled into ideas.

Unit 3

Mini-Beast Magic

'Hurt No Living Thing' by Christina Rossetti

Opening Doors key reading strategy: mood monitor

Can you sense how a poem affects your feelings and mood?

Can you write a celebratory poem with different moods?

Exploring the wonder of mini-beasts at Key Stage 1 has been a firm favourite for many years. From a science and local geography perspective, the opportunity for teachers to build respectful attitudes towards, as well as knowledge about, the natural world always seems to be at the core of learning. This unit aims to show how teachers can lift the lid on writing opportunity and challenge by using a carefully chosen poetic text alongside a science topic. Mini-beast units will usually include some descriptive writing that links observation to word choices. Christina Rossetti's poem 'Hurt No Living Thing' opens doors to young writers to create a mood of awe, wonder and celebration in the choices they make, going far beyond the mere selection of adjectives.

Access strategies

Organise the children into mixed ability groups (ideally of four). Assign one of the following mini-beasts to each group: worm, cricket, grasshopper, ladybird, butterfly, moth, gnat and beetle. Provide an image of each creature and ask the children to discuss what they know about their creature within their group. This unit works best when the class are some way into a science topic, so you can draw on their developing knowledge and the value and pleasure in sharing and consolidating it. If a group has no knowledge of their mini-beast, ask for experts from the wider group; where necessary, you could assemble a short fact file to share on some of the more obscure examples. The gnat can often be a stumbling block!

Ask the children to **think, pair, share** in their groups: what is the best adjective to describe their group's animal? Why did they choose this word?

Leah says ...

Although this strategy is well-known, think, pair, share ensures that all group members contribute ideas, which is then followed by a group task to evaluate the suggestions and select the one adjective they want to share with the class. All ideas are valued, but the children are inducted into a culture in which some ideas may be assessed by the group to be more valuable than others.

The groups should then share their choice, and their reasons for choosing it, with the class, which will give you, as the teacher, an insight into what the children understand by 'best'. This provides an opportunity to develop some shared evaluation criteria.

Now repeat the activity, insisting that the adjective choice celebrates something positive about their creature. There could be an example in the groups' initial brainstorm or you could develop one together. With a Year 2 class at Overton Primary School in Hampshire, the children made the change from 'black beetle' to 'ebony beetle' and from 'slimy worm' to 'curly worm'. The group discussed how ebony sounded more precious and rare than black, and how curly was not just more likeable than slimy but also more fun because of the echo of the 'er' sound in worm.

Taster draft

Explain to the children that by placing an adjective before a noun they have been making noun phrases, and that we can create different moods or feelings by adding a description after the noun:

Before ...	After ...
Wriggly digging worm	Worm that wriggles and digs
Delicate moth	Moth with delicate wings
Dazzling butterfly	Butterfly so dazzling

Notice together that the words *that, with* and *so* provide ways to add information after the noun and so create a longer and more rhythmic phrase.

Without labouring over the label of each grammatical structure, set the groups free to experiment with post-modification and to come up with a single line. Children catch on remarkably quickly when they can work collectively to draft and redraft orally. Now ask the groups to rehearse their line together, using a voice that matches the mood of their line.

Finally, ask the class to come together and perform their **taster draft** class poem as a group – at least twice! It would be great to capture the whole poem on a flip chart to build the children's sense of confidence that in only twenty minutes or so, they have written a rhythmic class poem with a variety of celebratory moods. Feel free to pause at this point and discuss where the lines make them feel different – where the mood might change. The poem by Year 2 pupils at Overton Primary School went like this:

Crickets so croaky

Worms so curly

Moths with delicate wings

Crickets so springy

Gnat with crazy wings

Beetle with ebony shell

Grasshoppers with singing wings.

Reading journeys

The children will now be more than ready to read the full Rossetti poem. We always provide an initial reading and then let the children take a line each in their groups and reread the poem in the round.

Resource 10

Hurt No Living Thing

Hurt no living thing:
Ladybird, nor butterfly,
Nor moth with dusty wing,
Nor cricket chirping cheerily,
Nor grasshopper so light of leap,
Nor dancing gnat, nor beetle fat,
Nor harmless worms that creep.

Leah says ...

We can too often assume that one reading of a poem is enough for children to build both meaning and response. The golden rule is that one reading is never enough! For pupils to explore the key strategy for this lesson – to monitor the subtlety with which different moods are created – they need to experience the many dimensions of prosody (or sound play) in this poised and prayer-like piece.

First, ask each group to discuss how the poem makes them feel about mini-beasts. Do their feelings change as they read it? Noticing and valuing differences in emotional responses is an important stepping stone to becoming an evaluative reader. Perhaps it should be our starting point more frequently for older readers too, as they begin to build the concept of critical evaluation.

Year 2 at Overton had been developing reading through **dialogic talk** for a whole academic year by the time we trialled this unit in the summer. They were well beyond setting group targets like including everyone in the discussion and taking turns. Instead, they set themselves a goal at the beginning of the lesson to share ideas for which they had evidence and not to say 'random things' – their words! When we reached the discussion point in the lesson, we linked back to this goal – to share feelings but to identify where this might have come from in the poem.

One group felt worried about the mini-beasts, which they linked to the line 'Hurt no living thing', as it reminded them how easy it is to squash worms and insects. Another felt this line was more calm: 'It means all the animals will have a peaceful life.' This combination of concern and calm stems from the religious, prayer-like mood of the command verb structure. One group contrasted this with the repetition of 'nor', which they said helped them to feel more cheerful because of its bouncy rhythm. The group which had started with the gnat were able to share how the poem had changed their view of it as an insect that bites: 'The word "dancing" makes you want to see it fly – it sounds unusual.' One group felt the repeated sounds in 'cricket chirping cheerily' made them 'feel more excited'.

The children were responding to far more than word choices here: they were responding to the range of moods in Rossetti's lyricism. A **lyric poem** is one in which the poet expresses personal feelings through strong musicality – classical lyrics were originally set to music. The children's sensitivity to feelings and musicality suggested that they were ready for the deep reading question.

Support:	**Support:**
Some creatures are just named and some are described. Why might this be?	Can you find any repetition of words or sounds? What do they add to the mood?

How does Christina Rossetti celebrate mini-beasts and their different kinds of beauty?

Support:	**Greater depth:**
Why might the writer have put the creatures in this order?	Do the rhythm and rhyme change how you feel as a reader?

As with all 'Opening Doors' units, it is down to teachers to sense the confidence in the room and observe whether some groups need the radial support questions to scaffold their thinking or whether they are ready for prompts to think at greater depth.

Excellent responses will include:

Key concept: creating mood through the music of language (prosody)

- The prayer-like seriousness and calm that comes from the command verb in the opening line.
- The feeling of safety (like incantation) in the repetition of 'nor'.
- The playful alliteration that introduces a note of fun and celebration: 'chirping cheerily', 'light of leap'.
- The end rhymes and internal rhymes which bring a song-like celebration to the mood.

Key concept: creating inferences through word choice

- The economical but precise choice of noun modification. The glamorous ladybird and butterfly need no modification, whilst the lowly worm is adorned with pre- and post-modifiers!

Key concept: affecting reader viewpoint through structure

- The careful ordering of the insects. The dusty winged moth is slipped in after the better loved butterfly and ladybird and is painted more carefully. Rossetti also chooses to include the least 'beautiful' insects towards the end. (The Overton pupils also wondered whether Rossetti was moving from the air to the earth in her ordering – though some were troubled by the gnat appearing where it does!)

Beyond the limit – link reading

All the poems below are about insects and mini-beasts and all include changes in mood:

- 'Butterfly' by June Crebbin
- 'Caterpillar' by Christina Rossetti
- 'Wasp on the Tube' by Chrissie Gittins
- 'Snail' and 'Worm' by Ted Hughes
- 'If You Catch a Firefly' by Lilian Moore
- 'Bluebottle' and 'Cockroach' by Judith Nicholls
- 'Don't Cry Caterpillar' by Grace Nichols

The works listed below are more related to the relationship between humans and animals; again, they call for sensitivity to mood changes to build meaning and response:

- 'Gorilla Gazing' by James Carter
- 'The Mouse's Nest' by John Clare
- 'Extinct' by Mandy Coe
- 'Alys at the Zoo' by Raymond Garlick
- 'Variation on an Old Rhyme' by John Mole

If you want to link to picture books that create wonder whilst they educate, you might wish to explore:

- ❧ *Yucky Worms* by Vivian French and Jessica Ahlberg
- ❧ *The Book of Bees* by Piotr Socha and Wojciech Grajkowski
- ❧ *Moth: An Evolution Story* by Isabel Thomas and Daniel Egnéus

Wings to fly

- ❧ Write your own mini-beast poem inspired by Christina Rossetti. Try to include changes in mood: how will your opening mood be different from your ending?

  A simple writing frame could be provided for writers who might need a stepping stone before they compose without scaffolds:

Hurt not the humble snail:

_____ snails that _____

Snails with _____

Snails _____ing _____ly

Snails so _____

Resource 11

- ❧ Write a poem to celebrate and notice creatures that are less obviously beautiful to humans, or perhaps are all too common and taken for granted.
- ❧ Write a poem to celebrate different aspects of just one living creature (such as an endangered animal), noticing all the most

precious things we are in danger of losing should they become extinct.

Here are some poems inspired by 'Hurt No Living Thing' by Year 2 pupils from Overton Primary School:

Beautiful bugs,
Even snails and slugs,
The ladybird's wings
And the cricket's springs
When the delicate moths
And the grasshopper hops,
Kind butterflies and beetles
Scuttle by when the worms
Wriggle gently and the earwigs
Eat earscreechingly
The bees buzz beautifully
Beautiful bugs.

Indigo Targett

Grasshoppers spring
Crickets croak
Ladybirds crawl
Moths dance in the air
Worms slither

Gnats crazy dance
Butterflies flutter and
Beetles scutter.
Aren't insects a wonder?

Freya Berry

No matter what you are
We're all equal by far.

Even gnats with itchy bite,
Even spiders that give a fright.

Although snails are slow,
And worms are low,
Everything is special.

Every creature has something to hide,
So try to find the bright side.

Gabby Macleod

How Out of Breath You Are

'Dear March – Come In –'
by Emily Dickinson

Opening Doors key strategy: personal places

Can you understand how famous poets bring alive a time of the year?

How well can you write about the special feel of a month or season?

Poets breathe life into settings, objects, ideas and surroundings by finding the words to which readers can relate. The imaginative scope in poetry is endless.

Samuel Taylor Coleridge, who wrote 'The Rime of the Ancient Mariner', called poetry 'the *best* words in the best order'. That is a short phrase which sums up what your pupils need to learn to improve their poetry. It is all about crafting, editing and innovating, but never losing the beauty of the whole poem.

There are many ways to teach poetry, but immersing young children in a variety of high quality but accessible literature lies at the heart of

it. Find the big idea, the enduring concept, the thought-provoking image in the texts you select, and, suddenly, comprehension and writing journeys can be deeper and richer. These ambitious objectives can be delivered using Emily Dickinson's poem about March – or any of the other poems featured in this book. They all teach pupils how personal views and angles on a scene or sound can be turned into distinctive images. As always, use the **link reading** to smother your class with quality ideas and questions.

Bob says...

Even a few lines of quality writing may stimulate more learning than pages and pages of predictable text.

Access strategies

Make a list of the associations your pupils might have with certain months of the year and support this with relevant images you have found. Allocate each group in the class a different month. Some months, like December, will be easier, so distribute the challenge as appropriate.

After some feedback on the list of associations, read out the beginning of the Dickinson poem to illustrate the way in which an imaginative welcome might be given to March:

Resource 13

Dear March – Come in

How glad I am –

I hoped for you before –
Put down your Hat –
You must have walked –
How out of Breath you are –

Such a rich text raises many questions:

- How does Emily Dickinson make the poem personal?
- Why does the poet hope for March 'before'?
- How are the dashes used?
- Why are there capitals for 'Hat' and 'Breath'?

Use the illustration to get the children thinking about how a specific month could be personified or represented in a drawing. Try using the link reading poems at this point. Which images might be chosen in a drawing for a specific month or season?

Move quickly to a **taster draft** in which the children must start their own stanza with 'Dear' and then choose a month. Encourage them to include an **imperative** (like the line with the hat) to imitate the idea of a welcome visitor. Some of your pupils may already understand that they could put all kinds of creative spins on the theme and regard the month as unwelcome too.

You could integrate some of the other slivers of text that follow at this point, or wait until after the **reading journeys**. Different methods may be appropriate for different pupils.

Personal addresses in poetry are common when the 'voice' of the narrator makes contact with the subject. You might find the following examples useful to show the children how inventive such addresses can be. This extract is from 'Words' by Edward Thomas:

I know you:

You are light as dreams,

Tough as oak,

Precious as gold,

As poppies and corn,

Or an old cloak:

How would your pupils 'speak' in poetry to 'words'? Which single word or image do they think has the most impact and why? You can find the full poem here: https://www.poemhunter.com/poem/words-2/.

Try a taster draft starting 'I know you' and ask your pupils to describe what words are like to them in their imagination. Encourage them to think about sounds, associations and the impact of different words. Younger pupils might prefer to write a few lines around a letter from the alphabet.

John Clare's sounds and sensations in these lines from 'Pleasant Sounds' may also help you to make more connections:

The rustle of birds' wings startled from their nests or flying unseen into the bushes;

The whizzing of larger birds overhead in a wood, such as crows, puddocks, buzzards;

The trample of robins and woodlarks on the brown leaves, and the patter of squirrels on the green moss;

The fall of an acorn on the ground.

Emily Dickinson led a sheltered life in Massachusetts, but after her death her poetry became more widely read and she is now regarded as one of America's greatest ever poets. John Clare suffered from depression and spent a lot of time in institutions in Northamptonshire, but he is now revered for the beauty of his imagery. Edward Thomas was a war poet as well as a nature poet – he died tragically young during the First World War. Encourage your pupils to discover more about the poets' lives using the links below as a starting point:

❦ Emily Dickinson: https://www.poets.org/poetsorg/poet/emily-dickinson

❦ John Clare: https://johnclaresociety.wordpress.com

❦ Edward Thomas: http://www.edward-thomas-fellowship.org.uk/home.html

Bob says ...

Introduce your pupils at a young age to the world of literature and you will be opening doors for a lifetime – with the right access, the earlier the better.

Reading journeys

You can now reveal the whole poem.

In trialling these resources, we found that some Year 2 and 3 teachers kept the focus on the few short lines that have been explored so far. The scope for learning about poetry was deep and the pupils responded well, but they may not have been ready for the whole poem alongside some of the harder concepts. The phrase used in Bob's tip, 'with the right access', is apposite. These resources are designed for maximum flexibility.

Dear March – Come In –

Dear March – Come in

How glad I am –

I hoped for you before –

Put down your Hat –

You must have walked –

How out of Breath you are –

Dear March, how are you, and the Rest –

Did you leave Nature well –
Oh March, Come right upstairs with me –
I have so much to tell –

I got your Letter, and the Birds –
The Maples never knew that you were coming –
I declare – how Red their Faces grew –
But March, forgive me –
And all those Hills you left for me to Hue –
There was no Purple suitable –
You took it all with you –

Who knocks? That April –
Lock the Door –
I will not be pursued –
He stayed away a Year to call
When I am occupied –
But trifles look so trivial
As soon as you have come

That blame is just as dear as Praise
And Praise as mere as Blame –

It is important to discuss the sheer delight of the concept of a month as a visitor. Ask the children to think about a guest visiting their home. What does the door represent? When do we ask someone in? How do we relate to the months of the year or, as in the poem, do they flash by too quickly, with the next month standing ready?

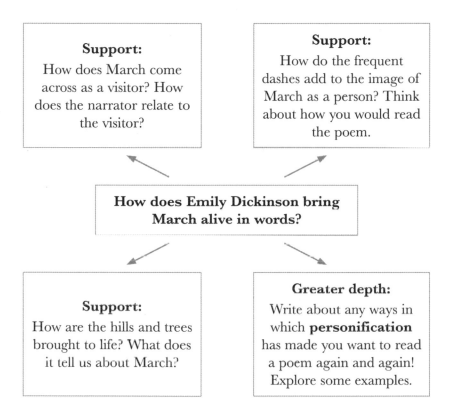

Support:
How does March come across as a visitor? How does the narrator relate to the visitor?

Support:
How do the frequent dashes add to the image of March as a person? Think about how you would read the poem.

How does Emily Dickinson bring March alive in words?

Support:
How are the hills and trees brought to life? What does it tell us about March?

Greater depth:
Write about any ways in which **personification** has made you want to read a poem again and again! Explore some examples.

Ask your pupils about some of the big questions of philosophy and thinking; we can only say that we are constantly amazed at the depth of their replies. Quality texts give us an opportunity to debate wonders and questions – and we are teaching our pupils the rigour of thinking and expression as we go. Showing how the dashes establish the interrupted thinking and excitement of the narrator is a good example of how the teaching of punctuation can be delivered through poetry – and with a far greater chance of deep memorisation.

The **excellent responses will** criteria, which have become a feature of 'Opening Doors' schools, can steer discussions within teaching teams to identify priorities for the whole class and/or guided groups. The **key concept** and **deep objective** provide the potential for greater depth, whilst the excellence criteria support teachers' discussions about top-class expectations. The assessment priorities can then be communicated in child-friendly ways as part of ongoing learning dialogues.

The use of pause dashes, along with other aspects of grammar and vocabulary, represent 'critical features', which Wayne Tennent and colleagues recommend using in their superb *Guiding Readers: Layers of Meaning* (2016: 43): 'The teacher will have considered the text potential before teaching and noted points appropriate for investigation. These points – or critical features – will be highlighted in the dialogue with the pupils.'

Excellent responses will:

As we advised in the introduction, aim to use these points to support the precision and depth of your teaching and planning, not as a dry checklist.

Key concept: punctuation for meaning

❦ Show how punctuation – including dashes – adds to the meaning of the poem.

Key concept: personal address

❦ Show how personification brings the image of March alive.

❦ Explore how colours show the nature of March.

❦ Identify the conversational style and how the narrator and March seem like friends.

It might help the children if you could find some images of early flowering red maples, which are common in Massachusetts where Emily lived.

There are opportunities for **music moments** too – for example, try listening to 'Song of the Lark' (March) from *The Seasons* – a set of piano pieces by Tchaikovsky.

Beyond the limit – link reading

❦ 'Poetry Jump-Up' and 'When Questions are Bliss' by John Agard

❦ 'Autumn Gilt' by Valerie Bloom

❦ 'Pleasant Sounds' by John Clare

❦ 'In Just-' by E. E. Cummings

❦ 'Stopping by Woods on a Snowy Evening' by Robert Frost

❦ 'November' by Sue Hardy-Dawson

- ❦ 'December Moon' by Brian Moses
- ❦ 'Child's Song in Spring' by Edith Nesbit
- ❦ 'New Year' by Karl Nova
- ❦ 'The Sea' by James Reeves
- ❦ 'January Cold Desolate' by Christina Rossetti
- ❦ 'Words' by Edward Thomas

Wings to fly

Wherever you and your pupils live, the months of the year will have some distinct associations. The access strategies will already have tapped into these connections, whilst the reading journeys will have taught your pupils how to develop new approaches to writing poetry. They can now apply them freely to a chosen title:

- ❦ Dear (___) – Come In … (choose a month)
- ❦ Dear (___) – Come In … (choose a season)
- ❦ Write a poem about a place which means a lot to you and about how it seems in a particular month.
- ❦ Write a poetic welcome to one of the following visitors:
  - ❧ Wind
  - ❧ Snow
  - ❧ Sun
  - ❧ Hail
  - ❧ Noise

- Music
- Laughter

❦ Write a poem as a conversation between a narrator and a month or a season.

❦ Dear School – Come In …

❦ Dear (____) – Come In … (choose a hobby)

❦ Show an argument between December and June

You have taught your pupils about some poetic techniques and you have recommended a range of poems for them to read and link together. The big challenge now is to get them writing in enjoyable ways to mimic the flow and originality of Dickinson's poem, but also to incorporate creative twists and inventive vocabulary. This advice from award-winning poet Kate Wakeling (2016a: 77) should help: 'For me, writing a poem is half about letting your imagination zoom and half about being furiously fussy to make sure every word counts.'

Voices in an Empty Room

'Green Candles' by Humbert Wolfe

Opening Doors key strategy: dialogue voices

Can you understand how a conversation in a poem can be dramatic?

Can you use direct speech in an original way in a poem?

Access strategies

Humbert Wolfe is an Italian-born British poet who was popular in the 1920s. His poem 'Green Candles' is a superb vehicle for teaching direct speech and the effect that the 'voice' of each speaker has in a recited poem. We hope you and your pupils will love the spooky atmosphere! A number of teachers have mentioned its associations with Disney's *Beauty and the Beast* and other animations. It is a very imaginative poem and has an ending which reverberates with questions.

Let's start with that ending:

> 'She shall come in,' answered the open door,
> 'And not,' said the room, 'go out any more.'

Organise the class into small groups. Ask them to come up with five reasons why 'she' may not go out any more and jot them down on sticky notes. Their answers won't just be guesses but will be based on all the stories they've read and films they've seen in the past.

Follow this up with a big question on a sheet of sugar paper: what has happened in the room? Ask pupils to note down their ideas. Establish whether at least some of your pupils can reference the story or film which has given them their ideas. Of course, you will get some totally original ones too!

Keep the evidence of thinking and speculating for later when it will support the 'wings to fly' sustained writing.

Now return to Humbert Wolfe's ending. How do the pupils think the lines should be voiced? Consider an emphasis on 'shall' followed by a very definite **imperative** on 'not'. Explain how this makes a huge difference to the reader's understanding. The door and the room are acquiring different personalities!

Now, reveal the first stanza.

'There's someone at the door,' said gold candlestick:
'Let her in quick, let her in quick!'
'There is a small hand groping at the handle.
'Why don't you turn it?' asked green candle.

The pupils will have to learn how to respond to dialogue in many kinds of texts – using a phrase like 'dialogue voices' may help. They will need to consider what kind of character is created by the direct speech and conversations. It will be a matter of combining the meaning of the vocabulary with the specific context and then understanding any inference or suggestion between the lines. These comprehension journeys are succinctly summarised by Peter Guppy and Margaret Hughes (1999: 134) as 'reading the lines', 'reading between the lines' and 'reading beyond the lines'.

Even in the stanza quoted above, there are opportunities to consider the implications of 'groping' and then to go 'beyond the lines' to explore our associations with candlesticks and the kinds of settings that a reader might expect. Of course, it's a green candlestick! What does that imply?

A richer English curriculum can be built on access to quality texts for all learners. Fascinating literature often gives the best possible opportunities for scope and depth in learning. A quirky poem with clever dialogue and fantastical elements, like 'Green Candles', can take understanding and imagination much further.

A **taster draft** will work well at this point: ask the pupils to write their version of the second stanza. Can they imitate the dramatic dialogue but instead use the chair and the wall as speakers? Give the children advice on how well this has been done as formative assessment.

You could also introduce other examples from the **link reading** section that will support the learning at this stage.

Reading journeys

It is time to read, enjoy and recite the full poem! It works well if different readers take on the various voices and role play in a large open space, perhaps in the hall or outside.

Green Candles

'There's someone at the door,' said gold candlestick:
'Let her in quick, let her in quick!'
'There is a small hand groping at the handle.
'Why don't you turn it?' asked green candle.

'Don't go, don't go,' said the Hepplewhite chair,
'Lest you find a strange lady there.'
'Yes, stay where you are,' whispered the white wall:
'There is nobody there at all.'

'I know her little foot,' grey carpet said:
'Who but I should know her light tread?'

'She shall come in,' answered the open door,
'And not,' said the room, 'go out any more.'

Note: George Hepplewhite gave his name to a distinctive style of light, elegant furniture that was fashionable between around 1775 and 1800. Reproductions of his designs continued to be made through the following centuries – one characteristic of which is a shield-shaped chair back.

Wolfe's poetry has been set to music by numerous composers, so for a **music moment** you could play Gustav Holst's *Twelve Humbert Wolfe Settings*, Op. 48. Why not get the children to make their own video of the room, with a minimalist, spooky set-up and haunting voices to complement the music?

A challenging text offers the chance to learn with rigour, but also with lots of fun and playful questioning. An in-depth question – one which involves much learning on the route to mastery can be useful. See figure on page 80.

The support questions can be set for the class as appropriate.

As we tour schools, we have found that some of them call the central 'Opening Doors' question a 'mastery question'. This does indeed set an in-depth goal for all learners. However, what matters is that all pupils are practising harder questions from an earlier age and sharing content and objectives. One teacher sent us an email saying that her 'low ability' pupils no longer felt they were struggling because they had made significant steps towards answering an 'Opening Doors' question, rather than being fed discrete and easy questions.

Support:

What do you think this poem is about? How does the poet convey this?

Why are the candles green? What do you learn about each of the things in the room?

Support:

How many different words are used to describe a way of speaking (e.g. 'answered')? Why is this important?

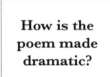

How is the poem made dramatic?

Support:

What is your favourite line? Why?

Support:

What do we learn about the lady? What ideas do you have about who she is? Why? How do we learn about her?

Greater depth:

What other poems that use dialogue have seemed dramatic? How was the drama created?

Bob says ...

A rich diet in English is the entitlement of all learners. Why not call them all 'learners' rather than 'high' or 'low' ability?

Plan from the top and, where necessary, use layered support questions – or any kind of intervention or scaffold – in a flexible way and with direct instruction built in. There are then so many potential teaching points en route.

Excellent responses will:

Key concept: effective dialogue

- ❦ Explain how each comment shows a new 'personality'.
- ❦ Describe the possible interpretations – and ambiguity – of the ending.
- ❦ Convey how the urgency of the comments builds tension.
- ❦ Explain how recitation of the poem enhances the meaning.
- ❦ Discuss the **personification** of the room and certain objects.
- ❦ Explain how rhyming couplets support the dialogue and meaning.

Bob says ...

Use the excellence criteria to clarify your understanding of why you are teaching the lesson. It is not just about delivering content; it is also a chance to teach aspects of poetry and language use. Sometimes, I've coached teachers in lessons where the literary material has not been mastered prior to the teaching. As a result, the learning can drift towards shallow memorising. Remembering is an important foundation stone, but a mixture of dialogic talk and instruction will take pupils' comprehension much further and much deeper. This can only happen when teachers have a confident knowledge of the text and its potential. This is the kind of understanding that grows each time the text is revisited and with talk across teams about the kinds of criteria used.

Beyond the limit – link reading

Make link reading available on desks and in classrooms. It is visible reading which will deepen the children's experiences. Make sure you have regular debates about which poems your class enjoys, both funny and serious, but keep using 'Opening Doors' strategies to ensure that what they learn is transferable. For example, when the class next has an unseen test which includes direct speech, they should be more discerning readers after exploring 'Green Candles', but they will need plenty of practice throughout the primary curriculum.

Here are some poems which include dramatic direct speech:

- ❦ 'An Off-the-Record Conversation' by John Agard
- ❦ 'The Night Express' by Frances Cornford
- ❦ 'The Fruits, the Vegetables, the Flowers and the Trees' by Carol Ann Duffy

❦ 'Overheard on a Saltmarsh' by Harold Monro (Unit 5 in *Opening Doors to Quality Writing for Ages 6 to 9*)

❦ 'Brian's Picnic' by Judith Nicholls

❦ 'Go-Kart' and 'Grumble Belly' by Michael Rosen

❦ 'Who Are We?' by Benjamin Zephaniah

Here is a picture book with poetic text and a deserted house story to compare with 'Green Candles': *A House That Once Was* by Julie Fogliano and Lane Smith.

Wings to fly

For their taster drafts, your pupils devised a stanza which can now be developed. They can start to apply their fresh awareness of the dramatic possibilities of direct speech to their own poetry. There are many ways to scaffold the process:

❦ Try crafting individual lines spoken by a new 'voice'.

❦ Invent a new object for the room (e.g. a broken mirror or a painting with a large frame).

❦ Draft a conversation between two objects.

❦ Devise an ending first.

❦ Craft a line using a specific verb or adjective which makes a difference (refer back to 'groping' in the access strategies).

These fragments of writing can then be edited and improved. Many pupils will be ready to compose a complete poem imitating the style of Humbert Wolfe. Here are some possible themes and approaches:

❦ Continue the poem in the same style.

❦ Write the lady's reply in three new stanzas.

❦ Write a poem including an argument between the white wall and the room.

❦ Invent a new room with voices but no human being.

❦ Write a poem set in the same room in 100 years' time or 100 years in the past.

❦ Green Candle Meets White Candle

The most important decision we make in our planning is about the texts we choose to teach. Our biggest debt is to the writers. Humbert Wolfe gives us all the inspiration we need for writing a brief poem which delightfully combines a simple drama with complex themes. Think of all the associations and connotations with dusty, neglected rooms, strange hands on doorknobs and ghostly voices, all of which take comprehension beyond the lines. Parents will love the voices performed in an assembly too!

Unit 6

Faceless

'Prince Kano' by Edward Lowbury

Opening Doors key strategy: only connect!

Can you understand how poets use associations in readers' minds?

Can you include common associations in the images you invent in your own poem?

Can you make these associations original?

Access strategies

Poets seek to connect with their readers' potential responses by using words and phrases which link with associations the brain already has stored. It could be that everything we read stimulates a constant interplay of meaning and interpretation. The more interesting the text, the more likely we are to have to work harder to understand it: our prior experiences of reading and image-making will be firing connections and correlations.

The unpredictability of such links in each person's brain is still a welcome mystery. If we teach using challenging texts, we will learn more

about just how deep our pupils' thinking and writing can go. Conversely, if our teaching expectations are too routine, those precious links may never be stimulated or formed for the first time.

Try asking your pupils to write down associations with the following words and phrases which will feature in the poem they are about to read:

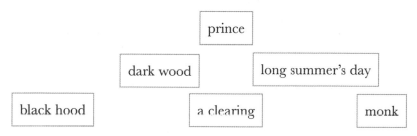

Ask the pupils to explore any associations they have with each of these images. They could be discussed using a **river of connections** from source to sea: the words are written down as they tumble down the river, with more unusual links or synonyms towards the sea – for example, monk:

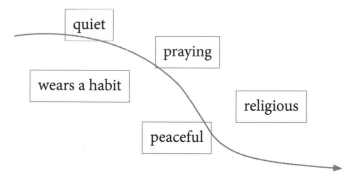

The key strategy is to 'only connect' between meaning and association – a vital stage in comprehension. You could apply a word river to any of the units in this book with powerful effect. It provides pupils with practice at playing with meaning, word crafting and articulating ideas. Too often, language exercises are divorced from purposeful contexts, but knowing that they will shortly see these images used by a famous writer will deepen the pupils' engagement.

In his excellent *Teaching English by the Book*, James Clements (2018: 54) writes about the importance of the depth of vocabulary: 'Effective vocabulary teaching needs to support children to develop the depth of their word knowledge, as well as simply introducing them to plenty of words.'

Bob says ...

Short exercises in the spirit of 'only connect' are vital in promoting depth and enabling interventions by teachers – for example, you may have to explain 'clearing' and some pupils may have preconceptions about the meaning of 'monk' or 'habit', which will need more instructional teaching to clarify their understanding. To get the most out of the tumbling river of words, aim for a range of individual interventions and productive group work to share findings, and offer some of your own contributions.

A footnote to this issue about connecting with previous word encounters is my relationship with the phrase 'only connect', which appears as the epigraph to E. M. Forster's *Howards End*. Whenever 'connections' are mentioned, I can't help recalling Forster's sentiment about the need to connect across races and classes and in an emotional sense too. It's a tiny example of the journeys with meaning, vocabulary and context which readers take with them. It's fascinating how the lives of words and phrases circle around us, sometimes only half-grasped. I think that writers like James Clements and Alex Quigley are right about the importance of word depth, so let's explore words in many different contexts. If you haven't read *Howards End*, perhaps now is the time!

Taster draft

A creative **taster draft** would be for the children to attempt the start of a poem or story using some of the connotations they have been exploring. For example, they could write the start of a poem featuring 'prince' and see what other links emerge. Alternatively, 'black hood' may produce some dark and sinister characters. Set a word limit (or time limit) to focus the pupils' minds and let them show you what they have learnt.

Are some of your pupils ready to go deeper with two important questions:

🐦 When does using an association a reader may have become a stereotype?

🐦 Do writers deliberately create stereotypes for a purpose?

Reading journeys

Give the children some feedback on their taster drafts and then read them the full poem of 'Prince Kano'. It can be useful to raise the level of anticipation before a reading. These kinds of introductions tend to work:

❦ I wonder what the full poem is actually about?

❦ What kind of prince will it be?

❦ How will a black hood feature?

❦ Are you all ready to listen to every word?

Prince Kano

Resource 22

In a dark wood Prince Kano lost his way
And searched in vain through the long summer's day.
At last, when night was near, he came in sight
Of a small clearing filled with yellow light,
And there, bending beside his brazier, stood
A charcoal burner wearing a black hood.
The Prince cried out for joy: 'Good friend, I'll give
What you will ask: guide me to where I live.'
The man pulled back his hood: he had no face –
Where it should be there was an empty space.

Half dead with fear the Prince staggered away,
Rushed blindly through the wood till break of day;
And then he saw a larger clearing, filled
With houses, people; but his soul was chilled,
He looked around for comfort, and his search
Led him inside a small, half-empty church
Where monks prayed. 'Father,' to one he said,
'I've seen a dreadful thing; I am afraid.'
'What did you see, my son?' 'I saw a man
Whose face was like …' and, as the Prince began,
The monk drew back his hood and seemed to hiss,
Pointing to where his face should be, 'Like this?'

Following the 'only connect' key strategy, it is worth concentrating on how the end of the poem reverses the expectations that have been built up. We assume the monk will be helpful and full of spiritual comfort, but in fact the poem ends with Kano trapped and comfortless.

Now try an 'Opening Doors' question with the usual support layered in as necessary.

Support:
How does the poet use each of the images we explored earlier like 'long summer's day'?

Support:
Which words do you think add to the tension – for example, 'Half dead with fear', 'pulled back his hood' and 'chilled'?

How does the tension build in 'Prince Kano?'

Support:
How do we learn about Prince Kano – for example, direct speech, emotions and settings? How does the punctuation contribute to the meaning?

Greater depth:
How do the associations of the wood, summer and the church compare with their use in other poems?

'Prince Kano' gives teachers scope to teach about challenging language, literature and poetry. Select from the potential **excellent responses will** criteria and note which of these the pupils are finding the hardest.

Bob says ...

If you pitch your interventions and instructional teaching at the hardest concepts, this will always involve recapping and revisiting.

Excellent responses will:

Key concept: linking images for meaning

- ❦ Explain, with examples, how we follow the stages of Prince Kano's journey.

- ❦ Show how punctuation – like the colon after 'hood' and the dash after 'face' – emphasises tension and changes the way the poem is read.

- ❦ Demonstrate an understanding of the surprise ending and how it comes about:
  - ◈ The direct speech.
  - ◈ The conventional address from the monk followed by the shock of the facelessness.
  - ◈ Our previous reading experiences of princes and monks.

Key concept: connect and understand

- ❦ Explore the way the connections with our associations (like the menace of the hooded man and being lost in a wood) lead our responses, only to reveal the hiss and the empty face at the end.

Remember, these are simply guidelines to be used in a **mini-plenary** as you assess the pupils' progress and to give you an idea about which aspects of the structure and devices in the poem you would like to teach more explicitly. A level of co-construction of these criteria can be achieved in dialogue with the pupils.

Beyond the limit – link reading

Select poems which also feature images or associations that trigger connections with the reader in unusual ways.

Statues in:

❦ 'The Watchers' by Joseph Coelho

❦ 'The Statue' by James Reeves

The sea in:

❦ 'Sea-Rock' by Grace Nichols

❦ 'The Sea' by James Reeves

❦ 'The Forlorn Sea' by Stevie Smith

Fruit in:

❦ 'How to Cut a Pomegranate' by Imtiaz Dharker

❦ 'Attack of the Mutant Mangos: A Fruit Salad Ballad of Baddies' by Andrew Fusek Peters

There are also many other fascinating poems by Edward Lowbury in *Selected and New Poems, 1935–1989* – try 'Unsecret' and 'The Storm'.

Wings to fly

First, ask the children to try making connections with key images. A simple image might be useful to start with, such as the universe:

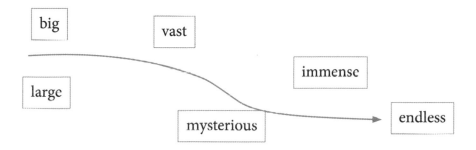

The river of connections can be developed into a fascinating language torrent! In preparation for choosing a title from the list that follows, you could devise some exercises on synonyms, antonyms, prefixes, suffixes, spelling structures or word derivation in the context of 'only connect'.

Try making more associations with any of the following:

- Dawn or dusk
- Holiday
- Queen
- Revision
- Scar

❦ Tower

❦ Wizard

It should now be possible to use some of these images in a poem which takes advantage of the associations in our minds. Like Edward Lowbury, can your pupils surprise us at the end by using an unexpected link? This is an ambitious success criterion but one which all learners can attempt.

Choose from:

❦ Princess Katrine

❦ The White Hooded Rider

❦ Invisible Women

❦ The Raven and the Wood

❦ The Round Table

❦ The Walking Stick and the Child

❦ Continuing 'Prince Kano'

Throughout this unit, the cognitive processes have been geared towards synthesis and comparative links. In *Tell Me*, Aidan Chambers (1991: 120) offers the following advice: 'all the time our experience shows that by finding patterns we make meaning, and that when we make meaning we are rewarded with a feeling of pleasure'.

Green-Eyed Scratcher

'Cat!' by Eleanor Farjeon

Opening Doors key strategy: shaping for sound

How well can you understand the use of sounds in a poem?

Can you challenge yourself to write a poem using sounds in a creative way?

Access strategies

'Cat!' by Eleanor Farjeon is made for dramatic reading! It provides an opportunity to teach about the ways in which **onomatopoeia** can link with the tradition of shape poems (or **calligrams**) to depict a savage and hilarious encounter between a dog and a cat. The rhyming of the vowels (**assonance**) adds hugely to the 'voice' of the dog – we are asked to identify with the dog's desire to scatter the cat from the mat!

The poem does not lend itself to an incremental, line-by-line approach. It needs to be read or heard in its entirety – your pupils must sense the overall delight of the dog's charge. However, the illustration and **link**

reading list will support access and comprehension. 'Cat!' is an unusual poem, and the fun and laughter provoked by reading it should support deeper learning about sounds and shapes in poetry which pupils can transfer to other texts.

Try using a predictions and puzzlement table to organise the children's thinking and language development around the image:

Predictions – what will happen next?	Puzzlements – questions

Now, link the resulting ideas with poems about cats and dogs using **quadrant boxes** to form connections.

Favourite words Why?	Favourite beginning Why?
Favourite phrases Why?	Favourite ending Why?

Bob says ...

Link reading means what it says: turning lists of recommended books and poems into part of the curriculum, leading to dialogic talk in your classroom. The effect will be electric! Make it into a wave of reading as the whole class go into the library and bring chosen books back to the classroom to extend their new knowledge even further.

After whole-class feedback, you should be able to teach the class more about the chosen poem(s) and have a measured vote on the most popular poem from the link reading list.

Beyond the limit – link reading

- 'The Mouse's Tale' by Lewis Carroll (shape poem in *Alice's Adventures in Wonderland*)
- 'Easter Wings' by George Herbert (shape poem)
- 'Next Door's Cat' by Valerie Bloom
- 'Footfalls' by Sharon Creech
- 'The Song of the Jellicles' by T. S. Eliot
- 'Four Feet' by Rudyard Kipling
- 'The Owl and the Pussycat' by Edward Lear
- 'Milk for the Cat' by Harold Monro
- 'A Cat Called Elvis' by Brian Moses
- 'For I Will Consider My Cat Jeoffry' by Christopher Smart

- 'The Kitten and Falling Leaves' by William Wordsworth (Unit 20 in *Opening Doors to Famous Poetry and Prose*)
- *Cats Sleep Anywhere* by Eleanor Farjeon
- *Thinker: My Puppy Poet and Me* by Eloise Greenfield and Ehsan Abdollahi
- *Mr Wuffles!* by David Weisner (picture book)

Reading journeys

Decide whether you will read the poem to your pupils with or without them seeing the text. They will be receptive following the link reading discussions, so, in this context, a dramatic reading with the emphasis on listening is a possibility.

Resource 24

CAT!

   Cat!

   Scat!

Atter her, atter her

Sleeky flatterer,

Spitfire chatterer,

Scatter her, scatter her

   Off her mat!

   Wuff!

   Wuff!

   Treat her rough!

Git her, git her,
Whiskery spitter!
Catch her, catch her,
Green-eyed scratcher!
    Slathery
    Slithery
    Hisser,
    Don't miss her!
Run till you're dithery,
    Hithery
    Thithery
    Pfitts! pfitts!
    How she spits!
    Spitch! Spatch!
    Can't she scratch!
Scritching the bark
Of the sycamore-tree,
She's reached her ark
And's hissing at me
    Pfitts! Pfitts!
    Wuff! Wuff!
        Scat,
        Cat!
        That's
        That!

You could assemble some line-by-line images and project these onto a whiteboard alongside the text as you read. This will emphasise the sounds and word variations that Eleanor Farjeon has used. A large font for 'sleeky flatterer', with a suitable cat in the background, would be effective, for example (but the images will have to be timed to change with your reading!). Alternatively, you could use the illustration supplied to flash up in-between the lines.

Children love interesting-sounding words, so capitalise on this by handing out cards with a line from the poem for them to read out. Go round the class to perform a group reading – and make sure to keep advising on tone and pronunciation. It's not easy! For maximum effect, encourage the children to reproduce the humour and the cat's fear of the dog.

To give the children a deeper understanding of the poem, start with the shape. As the form imitates the chase, there is a good opportunity to ask why there are single word lines and short groupings of four lines. A good place to start is this question:

❦ Why is 'Run till you're dithery' the centre line?

A table could be used to plot the stages of the chase. Here are some examples to get you started:

Words/Phrases	Meaning
Cat! Scat!	The dog wants the cat *out*!
Atter her/Scatter her	The dog's emotions link with verbs and action
Run till you're dithery	

A second question should now be asked:

❦ How does the shape of the poem reflect the chase?

Use the radial support questions (see figure on page 105) to initiate a learning dialogue. Some **didactic teaching** may be needed as there are new aspects of poetry which could be taught using 'Cats!' You could introduce the children to the variety of possibilities that sounds and structure can make – for example, 'Slathery slithery hisser' matches the movement and sounds of the cat to the meaning. It's onomatopoeic! The impression of the cat (in the dog's eyes) is expressed through the 's' sounds.

Much of this teaching will need to be repeated all the way through the English curriculum, focusing on increasingly harder texts and more intensive practice. As Clare Sealy (2017) observes: 'If having rich background knowledge is key to becoming a successful reader, then accumulating that knowledge needs to start as early as possible.'

Support:

How is the drama in the poem brought alive through the use of (1) assonance and (2) onomatopoeia?

Support:

Which phrases show that the dog hates the cat? Why are they effective?

How many images link with spitting and scratching? Write down your ideas in a simple table.

How does Eleanor Farjeon make the chase dramatic and amusing?

Support:

Explore these words/phrases for meaning:

1. Spitfire chatterer

2. Dithery hithery thithery

3. Slathery slithery hisser

4. Scritching

How good is the ending? Why?

Greater depth:

Explain how slang words and exclamations give the dog's anger a 'voice'. Can you compare this with a cat or dog in another poem?

Excellent responses will:

Key concept: shape and meaning

❦ Show how the extreme language is from the dog's point of view and builds a chase throughout the poem. It is direct, continuous and builds to a climax.

❦ Explore the single word lines and how the layout releases the frenetic action.

Key concept: onomatopoeia and sound

❦ Explain the use of onomatopoeic sounds and assonance rhymes – for example, the 'a' sounds on 'Cat! and 'Scat!' start a pattern which continues.

❦ Explain the spelling variation which produces expressions like 'atter' and 'git'.

Can any of your pupils show how the poem manipulates our perceptions of dogs and cats? Do we follow the flight of the cat with any sympathy, or does the style make us side with the dog? Is the dog talking to itself to gain self-confidence? Does the cat sound like a snake at one point?

Bob says ...

Teach spelling, punctuation and grammar in context. Why are exclamations so effective? Collect double 't' letters (like 'scatter') and double 's' combinations (like 'hissing').

*Capture the overall sound and meaning via the reading first, and then **zoom closer** to learn how spelling, punctuation and grammar contribute to the meaning.*

Wings to fly

Link what has been learnt about sound and shape with how this can be applied in poetry writing. Learning processes could involve:

- ❦ Adding more sounds and actions that the dog observes, using single words at first.

- ❦ Focus on 'slithery'. What other vocabulary could be used to show movement?

- ❦ Practise rhymes and assonance: could the poem start with anything else other than 'scat!' to rhyme with 'cat'?

- ❦ Practise a short section or stanza in which the shape matches the meaning. Search for more poetic calligrams (text which is arranged to form a thematically coherent image). There are some more shape poems listed in the link reading section.

- ❦ Practise writing a **taster draft** using the following lines as a stimulus:

Catch her, catch her,
Green-eyed scratcher!
Slathery
Slithery

Hisser,

Don't miss her!

The zoom closer method combines imitation with originality. Can your pupils come up with a different adjective for 'green-eyed', choose some alternative verbs and write a different summary line? If you provide plenty of assessment for learning on the children's drafts, this should build their confidence for a full poem.

Now, flood the page with poetry! Choose some of these titles:

- Dog
- Snake – write about the snake's movements from the point of view of another animal or human
- Run Till You're Dithery
- Cat Revenge – written by the cat about the dog
- Cat and Mouse
- The Boy, the Girl and the Puppy
- Home Alone for Animals
- The Nasty Cat
- Use *Mr Wuffles!* by David Weisner – devise a poem shaped for meaning written by the aliens about the cat!

You will think of plenty more – and so will your pupils!

Make the link from the excellent responses expectations to the application of new learning to the writing. The children's poems should show how sounds, action and shapes can all work together. The poems will be much appreciated in parent assemblies, on the school website and on the 'Opening Doors' pupils' work website – please do share your examples!

Part 2

Opening Doors to Prose

Unit 8

Foundling

'Over the Hills and Far Away' by Hilary McKay and 'Blackberry Blue' by Jamila Gavin

Opening Doors key strategy: syncopated stories or genre jazz!

Can you understand how one fairy tale can be told and retold in different ways?

Can you become the teller of your own version of a fairy tale?

Fairy tales are not texts that are authored and owned in the same way as most stories we now read. They have been shared, retold and adapted to suit the teller and their times – what we refer to as **syncopation**. What a true gift of inheritance to the student of writing! All great writers borrow, harvest and even steal ideas, but with the fairy tale this borrowing can be open and unashamed.

Leah says ...

What I mainly see in younger primary classrooms is pupils writing a rehearsed version of a fairy tale. Whilst this may serve to secure a story map and some language for later use, these exercises seem to stop before they become innovative and interesting. In this unit, I have tried to develop ways for young writers to innovate (or syncopate!) from a core story map from the beginning of their writing journey.

The foundling tale is less well-known than Little Red Riding Hood or Cinderella, so why does it deserve to be dusted off and retold? Because the foundling tale is always about otherness. A being, who is different, is found and brought into an existing social system – for example, a house, village or palace. The system might embrace it, struggle to understand it or even reject it.

A common thread in the foundling tale is that rejection comes at a cost – and could have been avoided. If that isn't a tale and a tune for our times, then we're not sure what is. Perhaps, in this way, fairy tales can offer a space in which we recognise the past and dare to imagine a future that is different.

Access strategies

Invite the children to complete this classic opening of a foundling tale by adding a setting:

Once upon a time, in _____ , there lived a husband and wife. The couple had no children of their own.

There are no clues in the opening as to where the story might be set, but some settings are more likely than others. Moreover, this backdrop will suggest something about the couple and the rest of the story.

Another way to explore this task is to hand out promising settings to small groups of pupils. Ask them to explore the possible inferences and then share these with the whole group.

Setting	What might this suggest about the couple?	What about the rest of the story?
A house at the edge of a forest	They live comfortably in a house, but it is next to the danger of the forest.	Will they venture into the forest or will something come out of it?

Setting	What might this suggest about the couple?	What about the rest of the story?
A cottage in the depths of a forest	They might love the forest and its creatures. They don't live near other people. Are they isolated?	Will other characters pass through and find them? Will they have to leave?
A house in the heart of a village		
A grand house with a beautiful garden		
A wooden house, close to the railway tracks		

Feel free to use picture cues to make this activity more accessible to all. Levi Pinfold's picture book *Greenling* is a modern take on the foundling tale, with an ecological theme. The setting is established immediately in the opening endpapers of the book: teachers have successfully used this double-page spread to introduce the idea that inferences about the theme and characters of the story can be deduced simply from its setting.

Now they need to describe the couple. Are they young or old? Kind or mean? How does this set up different expectations? Keeping the information brief but precise is crucial to the fairy tale genre. Try adding a relative clause: 'a husband and wife who were always fighting' or 'a husband and wife who loved each other with the weight of all the world'.

How about the final sentence: how do the couple feel about having no children? An extra challenge would be to link their feelings to the previous details about the setting and their relationship. If the couple are mean, they could add, 'And this was exactly how they wanted to keep it. No children, no trouble, and no extra costs.' The syncopation has already begun!

Leah says ...

You are inviting young storytellers into the reality of making choices. Lots of choices are possible, but creative writing, like any composition, isn't really 'anything goes'. Choices will cause ripples in the mind of the reader. You may wish to explore a few possibilities together before letting the children work in pairs to explore new ones, then talk together about the ripples created by each choice.

Now add the next line, which is the key plot device in a foundling tale:

One morning, they woke to find a parcel on their doorstep. Inside it was a small child.

Now you can introduce the term 'foundling' – a child or creature who is discovered with no knowledge of who left it or how it got there. Reveal that in a foundling fairy tale there will be something unusual about the child. This difference might be beautiful and engaging or it might be puzzling or even shocking.

Encourage the children to connect with examples they know from stories, picture books and films. You may wish to have some images available to support this process in case some writers are stuck for ideas. Again, Levi Pinfold's *Greenling* would be an ideal example. If your young writers don't want the foundling to be discovered on the doorstep, encourage innovation: is it found in the garden? In the forest? In a hole in the ground? In the branches of a tree? Can its location suggest something about the foundling itself?

The foundling	Words to describe it	How might your reader react?
Looks human but its skin glows	Glowing, luminescent, giving warmth	It is beautiful but will they be suspicious? Is the child magical?
It looks neglected	Thin, grey, limp, vacant eyes	They will feel sorry for the child. Who left it and treated it so badly?

The foundling	Words to describe it	How might your reader react?
It speaks a different language – or doesn't speak at all		

Leah says ...

This way of building story knowledge should have multiple benefits. Rather than telling children a core story outright, this approach values what they know and then takes them further. Together, they will be able to share their prior knowledge about how stories work. And because they have been active in this process, the shared innovation will build confidence in the community of storytellers as well as in their knowledge and skills.

We now have a story opening. The next piece of the jigsaw is to briefly explore structure. Ask the class whether the following would make a good middle and end.

The couple loved the child as if it were their own. And so they lived happily ever after.

This is neat and complete, but your readers are likely to feel rather let down. The resolution is just too easily achieved. Where is the struggle in the story? What kind of struggle might lead on from the discovery of the foundling? Ask your groups to think of as many possibilities as they can, such as:

❦ The couple do not want the child and find it hard to accept it.

❦ The couple love the child but the wider community is mistrustful of it.

❦ The child acts, eats and communicates differently.

The illustration in *Greenling* – with the husband and wife sitting on the steps of their house with the Greenling – would provide an effective scaffold here. The man's expression suggests he has already welcomed the child into his life and heart. The woman looks anxious and suspicious. Will the child divide their loyalty? Crucially, ask the children who they are encouraged to like and dislike in the illustration and where these inferences come from.

Taster draft

Your young writers should be more than ready by now to take the original tune and transform it into their own melody. Invite them to write the opening to their own foundling fairy tale as a **taster draft**, making deliberate choices about its setting, the couple and their relationship, and the foundling – its discovery and their initial reaction to it.

Share emerging examples with the whole class, asking them, as a valued **reading forum**, to respond to details in the story and to predict how the story might play out. Ask the children to share which characters they care about and how the writer's choices have made them care.

Reading journeys

Following on from the access strategies, just think how much more able your readers will be to make meaning from this opening to Hilary McKay's 'Over the Hills and Far Away':

There was a village, with a forest behind it, close behind, like a shadow. The village had an inn, and the inn had a doorway, and the doorway had a doorstep, and one winter's morning there was a parcel on the doorstep.

You can't leave a parcel on a doorstep for long. Not if it's alive. So they took it in, the innkeeper and his wife, and they brushed off the frost and unknotted the string, unfolded the shabby brown blanket, and there was a baby.

At this point, ask the children an open question which can be answered through literal retrieval but also invites inferences if you tease them out.

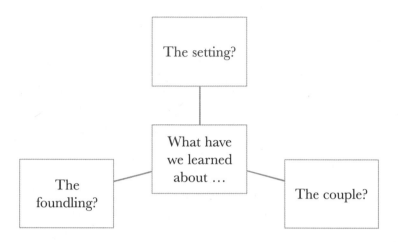

There is an interesting connection to the reading strategy explored in Unit 12 – tone metre. It is the mood, as much as the literal detail in the story, which offers the reader meaning in this opening: McKay's grammar choices cleverly suggest switches in tone. Ask the children to track the changes by reading this aloud together and finding a different tone of voice for each sentence. The ideas in the table that follows are offered to support your thinking, questioning and **modelling** – not as the 'right' response to the text.

Line	Tone
There was a village, with a forest behind it, close behind, like a shadow.	This starts out simply, but with the two prepositional phrases and the simile it becomes rather spooky — ominous but also intriguing. The tone invites you in and at the same time sends a little chill down your spine.
The village had an inn, and the inn had a doorway, and the doorway had a doorstep, and one winter's morning there was a parcel on the doorstep.	The list makes the tone quite matter of fact: 'There was this, and this and this ...' The parcel at the end of the sentence is unexpected — as if we, as readers, are tripping over the unexpected parcel.
You can't leave a parcel on a doorstep for long.	Oh, there is a 'you'! The narrator addresses the reader but sounds quite bossy and certain and, again, matter of fact.

Line	Tone
Not if it's alive.	This little phrase trips us up again, like the parcel. The parcel being alive doesn't fit with the previous matter-of-fact tone, so it seems all the more unexpected and quirky. This isn't a sentence: the 'if' clause belongs to the grammar of the previous sentence, so it sounds like a spoken voice, an afterthought, an overheard bit of gossip on the phone or over a neighbour's fence.
So they took it in, the innkeeper and his wife, and they brushed off the frost and unknotted the string, unfolded the shabby brown blanket, and there was a baby.	Here we go! Back to the brisk matter-of-fact, get-on-with-it rhythm and tone – but with a real live baby at the end of the process!

There is a playful gap between the everyday, commonsensical story-telling of this voice and the fact that we, as readers, are left with a real live baby on the doorstep: deeply shocking in a real-life situation but rather wondrous and intriguing in a fairy tale.

If you sense a confidence in the room, be brave and ask an evaluation question: is this a good opening to a foundling fairy tale? If so, what makes it so? If not, why not?

Leah says ...

Teachers often ask how to support children to edit their own writing, not just for accuracy but to improve its style. As with most writing processes, there are no silver bullets. Routinely pausing to think deeply, together, about the possible effect of choices, and then discussing this as a group, is what will eventually generate this kind of dialogic thinking inside the writers' own heads as they write and pause, reread and rewrite.

Now continue reading. Ask the class to keep this **monitoring question** in their heads as they listen: what have we learned about the setting, the couple and the foundling?

'It's not from round here,' said the innkeeper's wife at once.

'Gypsy,' said the innkeeper.

'Gypsies have black eyes.'

'Green-eyed gypsy,' said the innkeeper. 'Boy or girl?'

'Girl,' said his wife, unfolding the blanket further, 'Look! Gold earrings!'

'Never!'

'See for yourself!' his wife replied. So the innkeeper bent and looked, and sure enough, the baby had gold earrings under its wisps of brown hair.

'Someone will be back for it,' said the innkeeper. 'One thing to leave a baby on a doorstep. Another to leave gold earrings.'

'I shall say what I think when they come!' said his wife. 'Leaving it there for anyone to trip over! Half frozen too.'

The baby's wide green eyes looked at her. It didn't cry. They found out later that it hardly ever cried.

They gave it bread and milk, and a warm basket by the stove. No one ever came back for it, and so it stayed, from day to day, and then from week to week, and eventually from year to year. The innkeeper and his wife got paid a little for keeping it instead of sending it away to the orphanage. They called the baby Polly.

'A good plain name,' they said, looking disapprovingly at Polly's ears. Although they had both tried, they could find no way of taking off the earrings without taking off the baby's ears too. So the earrings also stayed. Perhaps if they had come off, they would have liked Polly more than they did; but perhaps not, because Polly was different. She was not like any child that had ever been in the village before, nor any grown up either. For one thing, Polly was not afraid of the forest.

The forest curved around the village like a heavy, green, growing threat. To the villagers it was like living on the borders of a dangerous unknown world. Except for gathering firewood on its borders, they avoided it. Some of the forest dangers were real: falling branches from ancient trees, hidden pits dug in the bad old days for animal traps, the possibility of being lost forever. Some dangers were less certain. The villagers were almost sure there were no bears, but also almost sure there really were wolves. There were probably no witches and certainly no dragons, but there were brambles like tripwires and poisonous mushrooms. The owls were eerie, large bats swept from its borders at night to hunt over the fields, while small, amber-eyed foxes slipped from bone-littered dens and returned with fat chickens clamped in their jaws.

Polly said, 'I like foxes better than chickens.'

This is writing ripe for exploring inference. The events are simple but the changes in tone quickly establish Polly as our hero and the innkeeper and his wife as suspicious and ignorant. Consider the stabbing, staccato exchanges between the innkeeper and his wife, compared to the calm details about Polly: her 'wide green eyes', her even temper and her lack of fear of the forest. Each paragraph is full of drama but ends with Polly's simple good sense. There is structural rhetoric in this device!

It might be worth pausing to explore the word 'disapprovingly' because its meaning anchors the couple's feelings towards the child. This is an 'ly' adverb, so it tells us when, where or how something is happening – in this case, a how.

In *Bringing Words to Life*, Beck et al. (2013) recommend the deliberate teaching of vocabulary, particularly when words are built from morphemic units that can be used to form many other words. In this way, we end up teaching not just one word but a powerful word learning strategy. We call this **word construction** because it helps children to see the building blocks of meaning within words.

This example gives us the opportunity to review why the 'e' is removed when a suffix is added to the root word 'approve'. But spelling rules are only one form of word study. Discovering how many other words are related to, and can be built from, these free morphemes (prove, approve) and bound morphemes (dis, ing, ly) builds literacy knowledge as well as the confidence that unlocks thousands of other words. Beck et al. also recommend that teachers help pupils to track a new word back to a known word or idea. This helps them to build webs of meaning, rather than single, unrelated bits of knowledge, which are very unlikely to stick without an anchor.

Synonym continuums can also be useful:

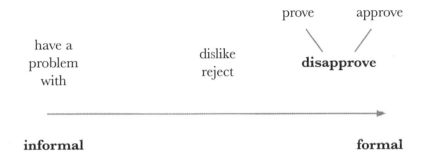

At this point, try to make time for some quick, oral usage of the new word in a familiar context (e.g. 'My mum disapproves of me playing on the Xbox. She looks at me disapprovingly when I am playing') and then in the new context (e.g. 'The other villagers disapproved of so much about Polly'). The meaning of the word is now much more likely to be recalled at a later date.

Back to the full passage. As in all 'Opening Doors' units, the aim is that one deep question about a passage can help to unravel all the little questions that sit behind it.

Your skill as a teacher is to provide opportunities for challenge, offering support only when it is needed. One strategy is to give all groups the **hardest question first** to think about together, which sets the pitch for the ultimate goal. As staging posts towards the big goal, each group can be handed a different **radial question** (see figure on page 130) to explore and then share their thoughts with the class.

Support:

What do you think of the way the couple talk about Polly?

Why don't they talk to her?

Support

What do the couple think of Polly? What clues are we given?

What about their choice of name for her?

How does Hilary McKay shape your view of Polly and of the innkeeper and his wife through the choices she makes in this foundling tale?

Support:

What marks Polly out as different?

How does this make you feel towards her?

Support:

McKay gives the description of the forest a whole paragraph. The villagers are frightened of it but Polly is not. How should we feel about the forest?

Greater depth:

What is the narrator's tone of voice and how does it change? The paragraph beginning 'A good plain name' is a useful place to start.

If there are areas that none of the children seem able to fathom, even together, then, of course, step in and invite them into new ways of reading by modelling your thinking about McKay's choices aloud, bringing the children along with you by inviting them into the dialogue.

Excellent responses will include:

Key concept: narrative viewpoint

- ❧ How the staccato dialogue makes the couple seem unfeeling and prejudiced but also ridiculous in the eyes of the reader, faced as they are with an innocent and abandoned child.

- ❧ How Polly's very differences are her strengths. She has guardians who seem to show her no love or understanding, but she rarely cries and is calm, matter of fact and unafraid of foxes or the forest. In short, she is both our main focus and our hero. We are rooting for her from the start.

- ❧ How the couple appear mean when they try to contain Polly's strength with a plain name, wishing they could remove her earrings and giving her a basket by the stove. They try to stifle rather than embrace her difference, yet it still shines through. Our sympathies are with Polly, not with them.

- ❧ How the gentle humour in the narrator's voice seems to stop us worrying about Polly: 'You can't leave a parcel on a doorstep for long. Not if it's alive.' It also makes the couple slightly absurd: 'they could find no way of taking off the earrings without taking off the baby's ears too'.

Key concept: inference through setting

🍎 How the dangers of the forest are given attention and detail to emphasise how all the villagers are afraid of it. By contrast, this emphasises Polly's matter-of-fact courage in the final line.

One possibility now is for the children to return to the foundling tale they began as their taster draft, syncopating it with deft touches of dialogue, humour and character and with a more detailed description of setting that links to character and steers the reader's sympathies.

As we stress in all 'Opening Doors' units and in all our visits to schools, the vital importance of **link reading** is for children to go deeper in their understanding of texts and concepts. This unit is about genre – how the same story pattern can be told in different ways. For this reason, we thought it was important to include a further inspiring and contrasting opening to a foundling tale: Jamila Gavin's 'Blackberry Blue'.

This time, the couple live in the forest itself ...

They longed for a child, but the years went by and no baby was born to them.

Resource 28

Some people would have said that the woodcutter and his wife were very, very poor, but they felt rich enough and, though they yearned for a child, they accepted their fate and didn't let this sadness cloud the happiness of their lives. Every day they went into the woods to look for food: they knew all the fruits and herbs of the seasons – they ate wild garlic in the spring, apples and plums in the summer, mushrooms and hazelnuts in the autumn and, before the winter set in, blackberries.

The wife's favourite time of year was blackberry time.

By this stage, the children should need very little prompting. How is the story the same and different? You can provide a grid (or even a Venn diagram) if a support scaffold is needed, but it is likely that the children will want and be able to compare the two couples, the setting, their relationship with each other and, importantly, their connection with the forest. As the children know the discovery of a foundling will be just around the next corner, they will also be able to predict how this couple are likely to react to it.

Offer this short introduction to the next extract: One autumn day, the woodcutter's wife drifts deeper into the woods in search of her favourite blackberries, but after many hours has found very few, 'reddish, hard and small' berries – no good for baking her pies – and falls asleep exhausted on a grassy bank.

It was a cry that woke the woodcutter's wife: a thin, plaintive hungry cry; a sad abandoned baby's cry. She sat up with a shiver. Everything was deathly still. All she could hear was the sharp clipped caws of the rooks, and the high-pitched squeak of the bats. The baby's cry had been a dream, she reassured herself.

She scrambled to her feet, feeling wobbly and chilled to the bone. She scooped up her basket, ready to go home, when she saw a huge rambling, shambling, prickly, thorny wall of brambles, positively glistening with the fattest, juiciest blackberries she had ever seen.

The woodcutter's wife rushed forward. How could she have missed it? She began to pick as fast as she could; so fast that the thorns pricked her fingers and tore at her arms, and her blood ran into the juice. There seemed no end to the profusion of blackberries, and soon her basket was full to the brim. Her fingers were quite purple, her legs were scratched, and her skirts were all tangled in the thorns. When at last she tried to scramble out, she found that she was trapped.

She struggled this way and that in her efforts to get free, but seemed to be caught fast. She was beginning to despair when she heard a faint cry. It was the same sound which had awoken her from her dream: a thin, plaintive, hungry cry; a sad, abandoned baby's cry.

'Good heavens!' exclaimed the woman. 'What's this?' She pushed her way deeper into the thorns.

And there, right in the very middle of the prickles and blackberries, cradled in the briar, was a tiny baby girl.

Her skin was black as midnight, her lips like crushed damsons, and her tightly curled hair shone like threads of black gold. When the baby looked up into the woman's face, her eyes glistened like blackberries.

'Oh my goodness!' exclaimed the woodcutter's wife. 'You poor little thing!' And she scooped up the infant and popped her into her large apron pocket. Miraculously, the thorns didn't scratch her as she turned to find her way out, and the brambles seemed to part as she backed, unhindered, into the open. Although she looked about her and even called out, no one appeared to claim the child. 'Well, my little berry, I'll just have to take you home,' she murmured.

The woodcutter and his wife loved their foundling child, and named her Blackberry Blue.

Readers are likely to pick up with ease the essential goodness of the woodcutter's wife compared to the suspicious and rather cold innkeepers in 'Over the Hills and Far Away'. What is interesting in this story is that the very woods themselves seem to be rewarding her goodness and magically bringing her to the child. This time, the question goes deeper than characterisation:

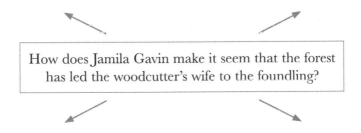

How does Jamila Gavin make it seem that the forest has led the woodcutter's wife to the foundling?

The question recalls Unit 12 in *Opening Doors to Quality Writing for Ages 6 to 9*, centred on Frances Hodgson Burnett's *The Secret Garden*, and the way that nature seems to lead Mary to the door.

Possible scaffolding prompts could be:

- ❦ Where are the signs that the woodcutter's wife trusts the forest and doesn't worry even though she is tired and lost?

- ❦ Consider the description of the baby's cry – why is it so rhythmic and so vivid?

- ❦ Compare the verbs in paragraph 3 (her struggle) to those in paragraph 8 (when she finds the baby). What do they suggest about the woman?

- ❦ Why does she not complain when the brambles tear at her and make her bleed?

- ❦ How does her reaction to the foundling compare to the reaction of the innkeeper and his wife in the previous extract?

- ❦ Consider the description of the baby: in what way is it both natural *and* magical?

Excellent responses will include:

Key concept: inference through setting

- ❦ How the wife feels safe in the forest, and it seems to reward her with the wall of blackberries.

- ❦ The forest 'traps' her in the brambles and then 'wakes' her with the baby's cry.

Key concept: narrative viewpoint

- ❦ She is not put off even when she hears the unsettling sounds of the bats and the rooks.

- ❦ She is undeterred even when the thorns prick her and tear at her arms – the language choices are harsh to show how determined she is.

- ❦ How the description of the baby suggests that she is an unworldly treasure ('threads of black gold') that has perhaps been grown by the blackberry bush itself ('her lips like crushed damsons').

- ❦ The language choices when she finds the child: 'scooped', 'popped' and 'murmured' are easy and gentle compared to the violence of her previous struggle: 'pricked', 'scratched', 'tore' and 'trapped'.

- ❦ Her exclamations contrast hugely with those of the innkeeper and his wife in the previous extract, revealing her natural, caring, parenting instincts.

The children should now have a heightened interest in, and connection to, foundling fairy tales. As Oakhill et al. explore in *Understanding and Teaching Reading Comprehension* (2015), structural knowledge is as important to reading comprehension as knowledge of vocabulary and the ability to make inferences are. The access strategies and **reading journeys**, which have built their understanding of writers' choices, as well as providing them with a basic story map, should make the reading of further foundling tales a pleasurable challenge.

Beyond the limit – link reading

- ❦ *The Jungle Book* by Rudyard Kipling: In Chapter 1 (Mowgli's Brothers), the wolf pack decide whether they should kill or adopt Mowgli the man cub.

- *Greenling* by Levi Pinfold: With the help of the Greenling, an older couple living in what looks like a timeless American Dust Bowl prairie begin to notice and love the nourishing powers of nature.

- *I Was a Rat!* by Philip Pullman: Bob and Joan, a cobbler and a laundry woman, take in a foundling that they discover on their doorstep whose only words are 'I was a rat!' Indeed, he is a rat trapped in the body of a boy. And so begins this satirical, mixed up, fairy tale muddle ...

Other well-told fairy tales can be found in:

- *Blackberry Blue and Other Fairy Tales* by Jamila Gavin
- *Fairy Tales* by Hilary McKay
- *Grimm Tales for Young and Old* by Philip Pullman

Pullman's stories are expertly and economically told, giving a grace to the original tales. In contrast, Gavin and McKay seem determined to blend and twist tales together for renewed delights, but their playful syncopations also disrupt some of the age, race and gender stereotypes that can prevail in the fairy tale genre.

Wings to fly

We hope that by this point your young writers will all feel they have the tune of a foundling tale inside them and have the skills to play their own melody. If they need some direction, you could ask them to:

- Develop their original taster draft using deft style choices and shifts in tone that guide the reader's sympathies – just like Hilary McKay and Jamila Gavin. Who do we care about and why?

❧ Retell the Brothers Grimm's version of 'The Foundling' using more subtle style features. They could develop the characters of Lena and Foundling, decide on the cook's motivation to be rid of Foundling or work up the symbolism of the forest.

Alternatively, you could offer a few open titles, such as:

❧ At the Bottom of the Garden

❧ The City Foundling

❧ The Rain Child

Here is some writing inspired by the foundling tale by a Year 4 pupil from Hordle Primary School in Hampshire:

In the dark, misty forest, a loud crash awoke a couple, who lived in a ramshackle cottage not far away from the mire. They were not kind and disliked everyone else. That's why they chose to live away from the city, far away in the forest. From dawn until dusk, every day they fought constantly, not agreeing on anything.

It was that night when they were awoken by the crash and it was that night that the foundling was discovered.

Peter sat up.

'What was that?' he questioned himself. 'I'd better go and see, it could've damaged my property, that could!'

Once he was up, he unlocked the door and stepped out.

'Just a tree, hasn't even touched the house!' Peter murmured, turning back. But something stopped him. Something wasn't right. The hole in the tree was glowing. He walked over then peered in.

He jumped back. There was a creature there, green and glowing. It had feathers on its hands which were stained with thick, red slime. It was gazing at him with fearful, distant eyes. One of its ears was damaged and flopped over helplessly onto the creature's face.

Charlie Dewhirst

A Power Struggle

'The Frost, the Sun, and the Wind' (Russian folk tale translated by Charles Downing)

> *Opening Doors key strategy: living nature*
>
> Can you explain and explore the meaning of this Russian folk tale?
>
> How well can you personify nature in your own setting?

Access strategies

In this beautifully simple story, there is scope for your pupils to learn about the use of direct speech and the way that personality can be developed through apt word choice. The **personification** of the frost, sun and wind lies at the heart of the story. We love the notion of jealousy and rivalry amongst the forces of nature. It is a kind of power struggle, with the wind getting the upper hand.

The key strategy is 'living nature', and once pupils are aware of it, they can apply it, when appropriate, to other texts they read. How does nature come alive in other texts in the **link reading** list?

Start with the illustration. Ask the children to write down suggestions about the separate personalities of the frost, sun and wind on sticky notes. Which words or phrases from your pupils' associations might be linked with each weather condition in the image?

The children could develop this into a **taster draft** along the lines of a conversation between the three forces of nature. It could be about:

❦ Dawn or dusk.

❦ Who is the most important?

❦ What trouble or joy they might cause.

The draft could be quite brief, but it will give you the chance to teach aspects of direct speech in context and introduce personification, perhaps through some of the link reading. Before reading the full text, your pupils will have practised the kind of speech they now need to understand.

Beyond the limit – link reading

These suggestions cover a wide range of reading ages and cultures. For younger pupils, the wise selection of suitable passages or poems can provide a fascinating introduction when they are not yet ready for the whole text.

❦ 'Wind' by Dionne Brand (Unit 1)

❦ 'To the Thawing Wind' by Robert Frost

❦ 'The Night Princess' by Jamila Gavin

❦ 'Frost' and 'Daughter of the Snow' by Arthur Ransome

❦ 'New Moon' by Kate Wakeling

❦ *Norse Mythology* by Neil Gaiman

❦ *Indian Fairy Tales* by Joseph Jacobs

❦ *At the Back of the North Wind* by George MacDonald

❦ *The Sand Horse* by Ann Turnbull

❦ 'Why the Sun and the Moon Live in the Sky' (African folk tale): https://www.worldoftales.com/African_folktales/African_ Folktale_10.html

❦ *The House with Chicken Legs* by Sophie Anderson

See also 'The Island of the Nine Whirlpools' by Edith Nesbit (Unit 14) for some further choices.

Reading journeys

Read your pupils the full text. You could stop after 'This they did' and ask them to give reasons for whether it might be the Frost, the Sun or the Wind that the peasant has greeted. Encourage the children to think about the meaning of 'peasant'. This is a Russian folk tale and the peasant's life would have been dependent on the weather.

The Frost, the Sun, and the Wind

A peasant was walking along a country road when he met the Frost, the Sun, and the Wind journeying together in the opposite direction.

'Greetings!' said the peasant, and went his way.

'Which one of us did the peasant greet?' asked the Frost, after a while.

'Me, of course,' said the Sun, 'so that I should not burn him up.'

'Nonsense!' said the Frost. 'He greeted me, for none is so feared by mortal man as I.'

'You are both wrong,' said the Wind. 'It was I he greeted.'

They quarrelled and argued and almost came to blows, but they could reach no decision.

'Since there is such dissension between us,' they said, 'let us catch the peasant up and ask him.'

This they did.

'Whom did you greet, brother?' they asked.

'The Wind,' replied the peasant.

'You shall not forget me, my fine peasant friend!' said the Sun. 'I shall broil you and cook you with my rays!'

'Have no fear, friend,' said the Wind. 'I shall blow on you and cool you with my soft breezes.'

'I shall freeze you into a block of ice, peasant!' threatened the Frost.

'Have no fear, brother,' said the Wind. 'There is no Frost, if I do not blow.'

Try structuring comprehension journeys around the challenging question and layer in the support as necessary. See figure on page 147.

You may have noticed that the 'greater depth' advice often reflects the need for intertextuality and extending understanding via links with previous concepts and objectives.

You will find that the structure of observed learning outcomes **(SOLO) taxonomy**, devised by John Biggs and Kevin Collis (1982), supports such learning journeys to excellence using five levels of understanding: prestructural, unistructural, multistructural, relational and extended abstract. You may find the taxonomy useful for all kinds of planning to open more doors. Most of the 'greater depth' questions in the 'Opening Doors' books reflect the most demanding SOLO level – extended abstract. See: www.johnbiggs.com.au/academic/solo-taxonomy.

Support:

Collect examples of dramatic direct speech. What makes it convincing?

Support:

Which vocabulary do you think creates personalities for the Frost, the Sun and the Wind? How? Can you write about the tone each personality is given in their speech?

How does this folk tale give nature a personality?

Support:

How do the Frost, the Sun and the Wind try to sound the most powerful?

Greater depth:

Which is your favourite personification of the frost, sun or wind from any of the stories or poems you have read? Why?

You could give key vocabulary to designated groups to deepen their understanding. A suggested focus could be on:

❦ Journeying together

❦ Burn him up

❦ Feared

❦ Broil

❦ Blow

❦ Freeze

❦ Quarrelled

Ask the children to come up with synonyms and antonyms or substitute one word for another. How does the meaning change? We call this **choose and change** to enforce the idea that an alternative word choice results in a slightly different meaning, inference or suggestion. Every word counts!

Words like 'dissension' are much harder and may need to be explained and modelled directly. Of course, this is the perfect time to teach spelling too: a lot of fun can be had with words with a double 'l' (like 'quarrelled') or a double 'ee' (like 'freeze') when matched with similar patterns. A focus on spelling is just one of many ways of teaching the overall objective: understanding the effect of personification.

In *Closing the Vocabulary Gap*, Alex Quigley (2018: 130) argues for going beyond weekly spelling tests: 'When we focus on explicitly teaching the alphabetic code, the etymology and morphology of words, studying and being aware of inflections, whilst addressing common errors with meaningful solutions, then we move towards a successful strategy.' We agree! 'Opening Doors' schools are having more and more success at doing this in the context of texts which produce the very spelling conundrums that need to be addressed in these kinds of ways.

This story is a translation, so it's a chance to explain to your pupils that different versions of folk tales appear around the world, and that we rely on the skill of translators like Charles Downing to enable us to read them in English. A tale like this one has been passed down over so many years that different versions have evolved. You will find numerous renderings of 'The Frost, the Sun, and the Wind' on the internet.

Bob says ...

Are any of your pupils ready to find different versions of this story on the internet and work out how the cuts or additions alter the meaning, compared with the Charles Downing translation? Even if some of them simply unpick the beginning of two or three versions, they will find it fascinating, and you can alert them to the huge difference that word X chosen as a translation over word Y might make.

Wings to fly

The aim is for the children to demonstrate an original use of personification and to apply what has been learnt. It should be exciting! Here are some useful writing tips:

❧ Add moon, sky, rain, cloud, snow and tornado to the possibilities. Ask the pupils to work on five or more suitable characteristics of personality for each one. The link reading should help.

❦ Get them to write a taster draft in the first person to practise personification – for example, Sky meets a large city. What do they say? What happens?

❦ Ask the children to imagine a meeting between their chosen forces of nature and (instead of a peasant) introduce a person into a setting of their choice, past or present.

❦ Role play the whole story of 'The Frost, the Sun, and the Wind'. Insist that the pupils capture the four personalities, including the peasant. Ask them to write about how they interpret frost, sun or wind.

Bob says ...

Drama is much more than just having fun. By taking on the roles, your pupils will learn to empathise and understand, to develop vocabulary and to transfer ideas to new stories. Can they capture the arrogance of the Sun or the intelligence of the Wind in their voices and actions?

Excellent responses will:

Key concept: personifying for meaning

❦ Effectively personify the forces of nature.

❦ Utilise single words or phrases to describe the personalities of the Frost, the Sun and the Wind.

Key concept: tone and accuracy

❦ Use direct speech in a lively and dramatic way.

❦ Use relevant vocabulary accurately.

❦ Introduce original twists and/or attempts at humour.

The excellence criteria are aimed at you and your teaching team, although the points can be shortened and simplified for your pupils. Conduct learning dialogues around the list: they are often productive. The criteria could be applied to any of the following titles:

❦ Frost and Wind Attack My Home!

❦ Sun Holds a Birthday Party

❦ The Mountain: Fire and Rain Row All Day

❦ A Folk Tale: The Revenge of Tornado

❦ 'I will make me a snow child.' 'But my sun child will be stronger.' 'No, my frost child will breathe cold like death.' Which child can you create?

Arthur Ransome (who wrote the 'Swallows and Amazons' stories) spent some time in Russia. His retelling of *Old Peter's Russian Tales* (1916c) will deepen your pupils' appreciation of the mysteries of a huge country where 'hardly anybody is too old for fairy stories'. In an introductory note, Ransome writes: 'Somewhere in that forest of great trees – a forest so big that the forests of England are little woods beside it – is the hut where old Peter sits at night and tells these stories to his grandchildren.'

Why not ask your pupils to share their completed stories outside and evaluate how many of them have captured the character of the elements? Years ago, I (Bob) used to take groups of teenagers on literary tours around the UK: the backdrop of a Scottish loch or a Cornish castle stimulated some remarkable narratives and poems. It seemed to release in the students a willingness to engage, talk and debate about writers and writing. Another colleague ran a workshop on the roof of the Martello tower outside Dublin where James Joyce stayed for six days in September 1904 (it is now the James Joyce Tower and Museum).

Literature can take us all, just for a while, to lands, real or imagined. If you can take your pupils out into an environment where nature is closer, then more is likely to be achieved as words and ideas flow. Robert Eaglestone says in *Literature: Why It Matters* (2019: 9), 'literature isn't just about the books on the shelf; it's about you thinking, responding, writing about, *talking with* the books too'. The more we do of this, the more we learn with our pupils. That's why we see so much daily CPD using quality texts – the ideas just roll, even with the tiniest of encouragement. The continuing part of professional development can go on in your classroom every single day because you are learning from your pupils' responses all the time.

Stories and More Stories

Granny's Wonderful Chair
by Frances Browne

> *Opening Doors key strategy: contrast collector*
>
> Can you explore and understand contrasts?
>
> Can you use contrasts in your writing?

Access strategies

Read the first extract aloud to your class – it is from a fantasy story, published in 1857, by Frances Browne, which centres around a chair that tells stories. Dame Frostyface is about to pass her magical chair on to her granddaughter, Snowflower.

Resource 32

'It was made by a cunning fairy, who lived in the forest when I was young, and she gave it to me because she knew nobody could keep what they got hold of better. Remember, you must never ask a story more than once in a day …'

Dame Frostyface set forth to see her aunt in the north country. Snowflower gathered firing and looked after the hens and cat as usual. She baked herself a cake or two of the barley-meal; but when the evening fell the cottage looked lonely. Then Snowflower remembered her grandmother's words, and, laying her head gently down, she said, 'Chair of my grandmother, tell me a story.'

Scarce were the words spoken, when a clear voice from under the velvet cushion began to tell a new and most wonderful tale … After that the good girl was lonely no more.

Ask the children to explore the following questions in groups. Give time limits for each question. Encourage the pupils to write directly on the text and utilise **white space thinking** around the outside to highlight ideas or ask further questions.

- What do you notice about the names?

- What kind of life is Snowflake living? How do you know?

- What does 'cunning' mean? Why is that important?

- For greater depth, can you say what kinds of stories the chair might tell? You will have to think about other fairy stories you have read.

Bob says …

If necessary, you can read the extract twice and ask for more detail after the second reading. There is a lot to respond to, so your prompts will help to take the children's thinking further. Pose questions which ask for evaluation and evidence. You can then teach the meaning of harder words in context. The fascination of 'cunning' is endless: we can associate the word with a fox or with someone clever or deceitful – but doesn't it mean a certain kind of intelligence too, worthy of much more exploration?

Your pupils will love writing the beginning of the tale told from under the velvet cushion! Limit the **taster draft** to 100 words, but there must still be a flavour of a fairy tale told by a magical chair. The subsequent assessment for learning can signpost pupils towards an appropriate style, if required:

❦ Did the storytelling seem magical or mysterious?

❦ Was there an original twist?

❦ Did the punctuation support the meaning?

Another access strategy is to use the illustration – perhaps ask your pupils how the chair might be visualised before showing them the drawing. Is there a particular kind of chair that might tell a particular kind of story? Is there an alternative to the velvet cushion?

Beyond the limit – link reading

There is a tradition of chairs being linked with storytelling, so some of the **link reading** could be introduced now:

❦ *The Adventures of the Wishing-Chair* by Enid Blyton (her first book)

❦ *The Silver Chair* by C. S. Lewis

- *How to Live Forever* by Colin Thompson
- *The Time Machine* by H. G. Wells

Other fairy tales or folk tales, showing all sorts of narrative styles and plots, will add to your pupils' growing knowledge and delight:

- *Russian Tales and Legends* retold by Charles Downing
- *Blackberry Blue and Other Fairy Tales* by Jamila Gavin
- *Cric Crac: A Collection of West Indian Stories* by Grace Hallworth
- *A Little, Aloud, for Children* edited by Angela Macmillan
- *Grimm Tales for Young and Old* by Philip Pullman
- *Cinderella of the Nile* by Beverley Naidoo and Marjan Vafaeian
- *You're Safe With Me* by Chitra Soundar and Poonam Mistry

Although *The Time Machine* is for older readers, visuals and very brief extracts may help to connect images and ideas in much deeper ways – it will be good practice for the contrasting which comes later in the unit. Try to use the illustration of the grey-faced boy in *How to Live Forever* to deepen the children's thinking about chairs and power – it is a superb picture book!

It's really a matter of adapting the sliver of text you use or the kinds of link reading you recommend to the pupils before you. If you are teaching children aged 6 or 7, you may wish to apply that thinking here and decide whether to use the tantalising introduction to *Granny's Wonderful Chair* or whether to explore more of the narrative in the extract that follows.

Bob says ...

We sometimes see a slavish devotion to a set way of teaching English which follows fixed linear pathways. However, without adaptation, synthesis and questioning the pitch of the lesson can drift towards teaching to the middle as the year progresses. We are suggesting that there are more opportunities for flexible methods and adjustment when texts with greater scope for learning are used.

Reading journeys

The next extract could be handed out for all to follow:

Resource 34

Next day, at sunrise, Snowflower oiled the chair's wheels, baked a cake out of the last of the meal, took it in her lap by way of provision for the journey, seated herself, and said, 'Chair of my grandmother, take me the way she went.'

Presently, the chair gave a creak, and began to move out of the cottage, and into the forest the very way Dame Frostyface had taken, where it rolled along at a rate of a coach and six. Snowflower was amazed at this style of travelling, but the chair never stopped nor stayed the whole summer day, till as the sun was setting they came upon an open space, where a hundred men were hewing down the tall trees with their axes, a hundred more were cleaving them for firewood, and twenty waggoners, with horses and waggons, were carrying the wood away. 'Oh!

chair of my grandmother, stop!' said Snowflower, for she was tired, and also wished to know what this might mean. The chair immediately stood still, and Snowflower, seeing an old woodcutter, who looked civil, stepped up to him, and said, 'Good father, tell me why you cut all this wood?'

The key strategy is designed as an open door to greater understanding of the whole text: 'contrast collector' can be applied to many other passages. We have found that pupils need more practice on close reading for meaning, not just exploring single words or phrases. They need encouragement to reread and consider meanings – and the best way is always to do so with curiosity. Finding contrasts provides a way into appreciating and understanding *Granny's Wonderful Chair*, but it may also open doors into other reading experiences.

Supports and scaffolds can be offered, as appropriate (see figure on page 160). The learning inherent in using support questions will be reinforced by a range of interventions and processes like oral feedback and **dialogic talk**. Challenging texts offer more scope for skilfully planned oracy sessions. Robin Alexander's *Towards Dialogic Teaching* (2008) has been influential in encouraging dialogic talk, which is also backed up by research evidence from the Education Endowment Foundation (2017). Voice 21 is another exciting new contributor to the discussion of the value of speaking and listening, both as process and product: www.voice21.org. Great teachers encourage dialogue, ask deeper questions and elicit more responses via lots of productive interactions.

The support questions should provide scope for a variety of group work. For example, if a pupil starts to explain 'creak', a continuation

Support:
What is Snowflower eating? What impression does this give?

Support:
How do we learn about the speed of the chair?

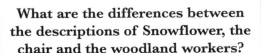

What are the differences between the descriptions of Snowflower, the chair and the woodland workers?

Support:
What do the verbs tell us about the woodcutters' activity in the woods?

How does the type of activity contrast with the images of the chair?

Greater depth:
Compare the descriptions of the chair with those of another chair in another story. How are they similar or different?

prompt to suggest other things that creak like a door will take the talk, and the understanding, deeper. Pupils can spur each other on around the class. Is oiling the chair's wheels funny? Is it practical? Use questioning to facilitate pupils' thinking – it's a constant process.

A diagram might support contrast collecting:

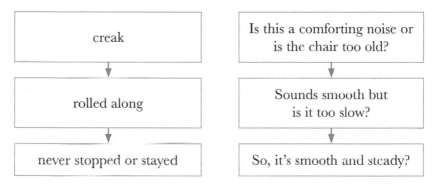

These images may contrast with or differ from:

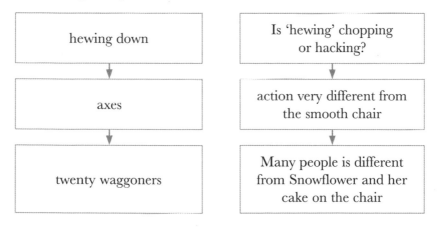

Find the right route to understanding which suits your pupils. Leave white space around the text and let them write in questions, like the possibilities we've discussewd, or place sticky notes around the outside.

Bob says …

If pupils can explore themes, patterns and links within a text from an early age, they will be more equipped to answer harder questions in formal testing. With lots of practice, more techniques will start to lodge in their long-term memory.

You might like to consider greater depth practice for some pupils by showing them more of the story and asking them to work on further contrasts – this time more independently. The same 'Opening Doors' question (from the figure on page 160) can be used.

Resource 35

'What ignorant country girl are you?' replied the man, 'not to have heard of the great feast which our sovereign, King Winwealth, means to give on the birthday of his only daughter, the Princess Greedalind. It will last seven days. Everybody will be feasted, and this wood is to roast the oxen and the sheep, the geese and the turkeys, amongst whom there is a great lamentation throughout the land.'

When Snowflower heard that she could not help wishing to see, and perhaps share in, such a noble feast, after living so long on barley cakes; so, seating herself, she said, 'Chair of my grandmother, take me quickly to the palace of King Winwealth.'

The words were hardly spoken, when off the chair started through the trees and out of the forest, to the great amazement of the woodcutters, who, never having seen such a sight before, threw down their axes, left their waggons, and followed Snowflower to the gates of a great and splendid city, fortified with strong walls and high towers, and standing in the midst of a wide plain covered with cornfields, orchards, and villages.

It was the richest city in all the land ...

The excellence criteria will sharpen your own expectations of potential answers, drawn from across the entire extract. This can be presented in any form you wish for your pupils to explore – as a list, in boxes or cut up into cards. The rationale is the same: use the statements for discussion, to guide explicit teaching and to spur on improvement. Try to avoid a tick-box approach as it encourages pupils to think that middle ground expectations are enough.

Some teachers also use the criteria to master the material before using the texts in lessons. Great teaching is constructed around the search for excellence.

Excellent responses will:

Key concept: contrast collector

❧ Give reasons for answers and explore specific quotes.

❦ Include the meaning of different verbs linked with the chair or the woods.

❦ Mention the impact of the direct speech, its differences and the choice of names used.

❦ Include, for greater depth, an explanation of the city and countryside contrasts.

Since you are striving towards excellence for all pupils in your school, why not link in your 'Opening Doors' inspired initiatives with a global framework for 'high performance learning'? According to Deborah Eyre (2016: 11), 'the best schools are reaching for high educational standards and use a demanding curriculum as the backdrop. They build the performance of students through access to a diverse, interesting and demanding set of learning opportunities that enable students to practise and hone these skills.' You can read more about Professor Eyre's research-based framework in *High Performance Learning: How to Become a World Class School* (2016).

Wings to fly

Try to encourage the use of contrasts in writing to make a link between what has been learnt and what can be applied in a chosen title.

❦ Predict what happens in the richest city.

❦ Recommend a design for a magical chair for the king or queen to use!

❦ Develop your taster draft into a story.

❦ Write a tale with a contrast between a magical chair and a magical musical instrument.

❦ How does the magical chair become a magical throne? Tell your story to a grandparent.

❦ Use any one of the following titles to introduce contrasts. They are all chapter titles in *Granny's Wonderful Chair*:

- The Christmas Cuckoo
- Lady Greensleeves
- The Greedy Shepherd
- The Story of Fairyfoot
- The Story of Childe Charity
- Sour and Civil
- The Story of Merrymind
- Prince Wisewit's Return

The text can be found at: http://www.digital.library.upenn.edu/women/browne/chair/chair.html.

Frances Browne was born in Donegal in 1816 and published many poems and stories, including this one in 1857. One of twelve children, Frances was blind from infancy but showed an extraordinary determination to read and write. In 1847, she set out with her sister to Edinburgh and then in 1852 to London, writing with huge industry and winning respect and patronage. In her preface to the new edition of *Granny's Wonderful Chair*, Katharine Pyle (2007: 4) writes:

All the sights of earth and sea, and many other wonders too, the old blind woman can show you.

And now she has laid aside her distaff and she holds out her hand to you. Are you ready? Do you care to go? Then take hold of her fingers and let us be off into the world of magic and enchanted things.

Unit 11

That Is Disgusting!

The American Woman's Home by Catherine E. Beecher and Harriet Beecher Stowe

Opening Doors key strategy: collecting words to build effect

Can you identify how vocabulary is used to build an opinion?

Can you use your opinion to create an entertaining review?

We ask pupils to give their opinion throughout the curriculum, but often we get little more than 'I like it' or 'I don't like it' in return. Providing evidence to support opinions can be tricky, so this unit unpicks the art of reviewing.

Access strategies

Food is a great topic and links to all sorts of curricular themes: you can collect data about favourite foods or food types in maths; consider wartime rationing or changes in cooking throughout history; look at healthy diets and digestion in science; draw a still life of food in art; cook, taste and develop recipes in food technology; find out where our food comes from in geography; and explore music and poetry about

food (see, for example, Unit 1 in *Opening Doors to Quality Writing for Ages 6 to 9*).

Quite often, children are articulate in communicating their feelings without speaking a word, especially when it comes to likes and dislikes about food! It is helpful to start with images for the children to react to, so collect some photos of very different foods – this could include a burger, chocolate cake, cockroach kebabs, leafy green salad and so on. Ask the pupils to demonstrate what their faces might look like if they were asked to eat each food.

Now let's think about our favourite meals. What are they? Encourage the children to consider where they eat the meal, who makes it, how it is served and why they think it is special. Now do the opposite: what is the worst meal they have ever eaten? This will really get the class talking.

Now it is time to work on word level by reading and collecting antonyms. Challenge your pupils to read and sort reaction words into positives and negatives – there are some examples you could try on page 170. Don't be put off by tricky words here. Recall how many children come into school knowing highly complex words such as Tyrannosaurus rex and Stegosaurus. Many children take great delight in the challenge of using exciting new vocabulary and, of course, you can explore phonetic rules such as the common 'ed' suffix or 'igh' in light and fright.

☺	☹
Excited	Dismayed
Elated	Appalled
Euphoric	Nauseated
Overjoyed	Repulsed
Delighted	Revolted
Ecstatic	Frightful

Extend this by experimenting with adding some adverbs such as:

I was *surprisingly* excited.

We were *extremely* dismayed.

They were *completely* revolted.

Verity says ...

In many schools, vocabulary continues to be taught as a list of words to be tested each week. This means that learners, at best, get frustrated at not knowing how to use new language and, at worst, see no point in bothering to engage in this seemingly pointless exercise. As a teacher, *you will need to model word use as well as give guidance when it is not quite right. If the children are confident enough to take risks with their vocabulary choices, then great leaps can be made towards deeper learning.*

Reading journeys

Having warmed up to words, share the following extract from *The American Woman's Home*. We find that acting out this passage works really well. Bring various sized potatoes into the classroom and make a show of how Biddy cooks them.

A good roasted potato is a delicacy worth a dozen compositions of the cook-book; yet when we ask for it, what burnt, shriveled abortions are presented to us! Biddy rushes to her potato-basket and pours out two dozen of different sizes, some having in them three times the amount of matter of others. These being washed, she tumbles them into her oven at a leisure interval, and there lets them lie till it is time to serve breakfast, whenever that may be. As a result, if the largest are cooked, the smallest are presented in cinders, and the intermediate sizes are withered and watery. Nothing is so utterly ruined by a few moments of overdoing. That which at the right moment was plump with mealy richness, a quarter of an hour later shrivels and becomes watery – and it is in this state that roast potatoes are most frequently served.

Verity says ...

*This is a tricky read. However, **modelling** reading enables you to use more challenging texts and scaffold the learning for all. Showing children how you stop to think about the meaning of a new word, use induction or ask a question about what is going on are essential if we are going to support metacognition. By using your questioning skills and allowing time for discussion, your pupils will be empowered to have a go at less demanding texts on their own.*

Encourage the pupils to think about how the authors have created such a strong image of ruined roast potatoes. Together, highlight all of the negative words which make up the **semantic field** – the group of words that build up the feeling and imagery. These include *burnt, shriveled, cinders, withered, watery, utterly ruined* and *overdoing*.

Get the children writing early and writing fast. Ask them to test their understanding of semantic field by using a short extract from Hans Christian Andersen's *The Little Match Girl*. As the poor waif sits freezing on the pavement, she gazes through a window and sees a delicious Christmas spread on the table of a wealthy family. As a **taster draft**, can the children identify the words that conjure up the mouth-watering Christmas dinner from these two sentences and then change them to create a more unpalatable scene?

On the table a snow-white cloth was spread, and on it stood a shining dinner service. The roast goose steamed gloriously, stuffed with apples and prunes.

Resource 38

Year 3 pupils at Westbury Park Primary School in Bristol created the following example when they combined their ideas in some shared writing – the addition of the eyeball is particularly distasteful!

On the table a weary, dusty, dirty cloth was spread. Upon it stood a cracked and chipped dinner service. The poorly cooked poultry was nauseating because of the wretched smell of the burnt, shrivelled bird, stuffed with a watering cod's eyeball.

As we saw with Biddy and her potatoes, role play can be a marvellous gateway into talk. As a class, watch clips from food programmes such as *The Great British Bake Off* and *MasterChef*. The children can make a list of the language used by the judges and competitors. They can then act out some culinary disasters and give feedback in the style of their favourite judge. Challenge them to use the vocabulary you have already collected, and provide sentence starters to ensure that high quality talk becomes the scaffold for high quality writing. Here are some examples to get you started:

- I was surprised to see …
- Ordinarily I would not expect …
- Who would have thought you could …
- Never before have I seen …
- The taste/texture reminds me of …
- Possibly your biggest mistake was …
- Nobody wants …

Reviewing food is a skill which usually mixes the bad with the good. Having worked through some oral rehearsal, return to this extract from *The American Woman's Home* where, once again, modelled reading will be essential. Before you read it to the children, take a moment and ask them to think about all of the things you need butter for in cooking – from the simple delights of bread and butter through to melt-in-the-mouth buttery pastry.

You turn from your dreadful half-slice of bread, which fills your mouth with bitterness, to your beef-steak, which proves virulent with the same poison; you think to take refuge in vegetable diet, and find the butter in the string-beans, and polluting the innocence of early peas; it is in the corn, in the succotash, in the squash; the beets swim in it, the onions have it poured over them. Hungry and miserable, you think to solace yourself at the dessert; but the pastry is cursed, the cake is acrid with the same plague. You are ready to howl with despair. …

Yet the process of making good butter is a very simple one. To keep the cream in a perfectly pure, cool atmosphere, to churn while it is yet sweet, to work out the buttermilk thoroughly, and to add salt with such discretion as not to ruin the fine, delicate flavor of the fresh cream – all this is quite simple, so simple that one wonders at thousands and millions of pounds of butter yearly manufactured which are merely a hobgoblin bewitchment of cream into foul and loathsome poisons.

Your question to deepen understanding might be:

Support:

How has imagery been used?

Support:

What techniques do the writers use to build up a sense of despair?

Why might the writers have used personal experience in the first paragraph, but not in the second?

How do the authors make butter seem quite so unappealing?

Support:

Can you collect adjectives from the text and sort them into positive and negative? How has this vocabulary choice helped?

Greater depth:

Explore and explain key phrases: 'virulent with the same poison', 'polluting the innocence', 'solace yourself', 'acrid with the same plague'.

Excellent responses will:

Key concept: identifying synonyms and antonyms

❦ Explain how a sense of disgust is created through vocabulary choice.

❦ Describe the detailed build-up of disasters.

Key concept: building effect through structure

❦ Explain how the narrative voice being directed at 'you' demands that the reader empathises with the situation.

❦ Discuss contrasting paragraphs: the simplicity of the food outlined in the first paragraph versus the details of disaster in the second paragraph. The comparison and shift highlights the awfulness.

In response to this reading, Florence Plant (Year 3) from Westbury Park Primary School wrote of her outrage at the ruination of some raspberries:

Unfortunately, a lot of people do not prepare raspberries well. You go to the table and expect a lovely bowl of ripe, juicy fruit but instead get revolting raspberries. Shrivelled up. You feel disgusted.

Verity says ...

Fully immersing children in the learning often gets much more out of them and can make what could be a rather dry lesson really come alive. This unit lends itself to having a go at making butter – simply whisking up some cream until it splits into butter and buttermilk. The children could then design their own sandwiches and have a tasting session that could link food technology and English. Instruction writing is a logical link to make here.

Beyond the limit – link reading

Select the most appropriate **link reading** for your pupils. Ask them to identify the semantic fields and compare the language used – perhaps a direct comparison of J. K. Rowling's butterbeer from the 'Harry Potter' series could be made with Miss Haversham's decaying cake in *Great Expectations*. Or you could encourage the pupils to think about what the White Witch in C. S. Lewis' *The Lion, the Witch, and the Wardrobe* would feed them to get them to tell the truth – Turkish delight seemed to work for Edmund!

- ❧ Why not visit the Mad Hatter's tea-party in *Alice Adventures in Wonderland* and review the perpetual tea time treats?

- ❧ Read Proust's wonderful description of taking tea and cake, and its effect on mind and body, in the first volume of *In Search of Lost Time*. What foods have such effects on you?

- ❧ Could you imagine being 'desperate with hunger and reckless with misery' like Oliver Twist in the Dickens classic? What would you dream of eating – cold jelly and custard?

- ❧ An entire chapter of Herman Melville's *Moby Dick* is dedicated to piping hot clam and cod chowder – the acute hunger of the seafarers being finally satisfied.

- ❧ Consider the mouth-watering descriptions of raclette cooked over an open fire in Johanna Spyri's *Heidi*.

- ❧ Discuss Jing-Mei Woo's experiences of Chinese New Year in Amy Tan's *The Joy Luck Club* when she realises that Chinese mothers show they love their children, 'not through hugs and kisses but with stern offerings of steamed dumplings, duck's gizzards, and crab'. How do different festivals and cultures use food?

These readings can be incorporated into all sorts of cross-curricular enquiries – for example, the role of food in festivals (RE), the feeding of the poor in Victorian workhouses (history), the effects of unsustainable fishing or stories about the origins of herbs and spices (history, geography, personal and social education, education for sustainable development and global citizenship).

Wings to fly

The pupils should have learnt enough about vocabulary choice and creating a semantic field for them to return to their initial taster drafts with a critical eye and redraft to tasty perfection.

Alternatively, why not dip into H. G. Wells' *The Food of the Gods and How It Came to Earth*, which offers a fantastic way into writing imaginative food reviews. In this tale, some chickens have been fed a secret potion at an experimental farm. This has made them enormous and at this point in the story they have escaped.

The chief immediate reaction of this astonishing irruption of gigantic poultry upon the human mind was to arouse an extraordinary passion to whoop and run and throw things, and in quite a little time almost all the available manhood of Hickleybrow, and several ladies, were out with a remarkable assortment of flappish and whangable articles in hand – to commence the scooting of the giant hens. They drove them into Urshot, where there was a rural fête, and Urshot took them as the crowning glory of a happy day. They began to be shot at near Findon Beeches, but at first only with a rook rifle. Of course birds of that size could absorb an unlimited quantity of small shot without inconvenience.

Ask the pupils to imagine they are eating one of these gigantic chickens, or perhaps another food which has been transformed by a secret potion, and write an entertaining review of what the food tastes like, remembering how to build the sense of disgust or delight.

Alternatively, develop some related non-fiction texts and oracy experiences. Here are some possible projects:

❦ Write and film your very own *Great British Bake Off* style episode – with dialogue dripping with opinion.

❦ Write instructions on how to cook some of the delicious morsels you have read about.

- ❧ Explain the changes in state and reversible/irreversible processes that occur during cooking.
- ❧ Persuade the catering department to cook your favourite meal/ pudding.
- ❧ Find out and write about food allergies in an informative text.

Unit 12

Shadow in a Drawer

Peter Pan by J. M. Barrie

Opening Doors key strategy: tone metre

How does J. M. Barrie introduce us to Peter Pan?

Can you develop effective techniques for writing imaginatively about a shadow?

Access strategies

The story of Peter Pan is well known to most children, so why not start by saying nothing at all about the text you are going to use or the objectives. Instead, display the key passage about the shadow on the interactive whiteboard:

She returned to the nursery, and found Nana with something in her mouth, which proved to be the boy's shadow. As he leapt at the window Nana had closed it quickly, too late to catch him, but his shadow had not had time to get out; slam went the window and snapped it off. ...

But unfortunately Mrs Darling could not leave it hanging out at the window; it looked so like the washing and lowered the whole tone of the house. ...

She decided to roll the shadow up and put it away carefully in a drawer, until a fitting opportunity came for telling her husband. Ah me!

We know from this taster that we are ready for something funny, strange and original!

This unit is going to give your pupils an opportunity to measure, identify and understand the way a writer can establish a certain tone in a story. We've termed the key strategy 'tone metre' to indicate that we are going to explore a famous story with our pupils and begin to get them to understand how a reader can gauge the tone.

It is through this method that J. M. Barrie both entertains us with a fantasy and also develops a dramatic and threatening tone. That is quite an achievement! Your pupils can start to learn how he does it in simple ways first. This understanding will go on to support a more sophisticated appreciation of media and literary texts as the school journey progresses.

Ask the children to search the passage for meaning using these questions:

- ❦ Who is Nana? Do you notice anything unusual about Nana's actions?

- ❦ What else is unexpected?

They could use different coloured pens for any evidence they can find for each answer or note words or phrases on sticky notes – answering questions fully can come later. Try to maintain their engagement with the text and with the learning. If they consider the tone first, they will then start to become enthralled by the language!

A table which lists the 'unexpected' sentence by sentence will help any pupils who are stuck.

Sentence	The unexpected
She returned to the nursery, and found Nana with something in her mouth, which proved to be the boy's shadow.	How can a shadow be in a dog's mouth?
As he leapt at the window Nana had closed it quickly, too late to catch him, but his shadow had not had time to get out; slam went the window and snapped it off.	
But unfortunately Mrs Darling could not leave it hanging out at the window; it looked so like the washing and lowered the whole tone of the house.	

Sentence	The unexpected
She decided to roll the shadow up and put it away carefully in a drawer, until a fitting opportunity came for telling her husband. Ah me!	

You may need to explain and explore the meaning of tone, perhaps by comparing this passage with one of the suggested **link reading** texts. It may only be possible for the children to reach an understanding by comparing and contrasting a tone of humour with one of threat, sadness or formality. By beginning to teach what we have called tone metre, your pupils will be able to recognise tone in other texts with more confidence.

This kind of interaction with the text will help to build literary skills for the long term. In *Making Every English Lesson Count*, Andy Tharby (2017: 19) emphasises the importance of continuity and progression: 'reminding students to use literary terminology when writing about a GCSE text is only possible if they have studied these features in depth in the preceding years'.

Bob says ...

Try to build explorations of tone through Key Stages 1 and 2. Do your pupils lose marks in formal tests and SATs because they understand surface information but not suggestion, innuendo or inference? If so, choosing challenging texts with fascinating tone changes will help, but like Peter Pan, this should always be in a context of fun and curiosity.

Now reveal the illustration:

❧ How does the illustration support the tone of the passage?

❧ Predict what might happen next …

Assess progress and decide what kinds of knowledge you need to offer the pupils to take their understanding deeper. For example:

❧ Explain how the action, seen from Mrs Darling's perspective, helps us to understand her personality.

❧ Highlight the matter-of-fact way in which the shadow is mentioned. It seems like an item of clothing being rolled up and put away in a drawer! The same applies to Nana – the dog seems to be almost human!

❧ Explore the tone of the neighbourhood. You might want to explore the phrase **tongue in cheek**.

❧ J. M. Barrie is creating a style within which the Neverland fantasy can proceed and be accepted by the reader. The light-hearted tone means that any threat in the narrative can be read by children without fear, although the drama is still tangible.

Before reading the longer extract, a **taster draft** will challenge your pupils to start experimenting with tone. Ask them to write (in 75 words only) about a different way in which Mrs Darling could have dealt with the shadow.

Excellent responses will include some of the same humorous tone found in J. M. Barrie's writing.

Here is an example by a pupil from The Brent Primary School:

Peter's Shadow

There was a twinkling, golden light following on behind him, which rapidly bolted about the room like a living creature. Suddenly, this caught Wendy's eye. One of the drawers began to shake furiously. Whilst the peculiar boy was rummaging around the wardrobe, she approached the drawer cautiously. Suddenly, the light raced into the keyhole like a shooting star and dragged a dark shadow out. The boy was overjoyed to be reunited with his shadow, so he instantly sped to the bathroom for a bar of soap in the hope of reattaching it. Frantically scrubbing the sole of his shoe with the soap, he tried and tried, without success – the shadow just slid off his shoe!

Beyond the limit – link reading

It is critical to link the **deep objectives** being taught with the whole text reading. Long-term comprehension is inevitably conditioned by the vocabulary encountered in every aspect of life. Take the phrase 'lowering the whole tone': it can only be understood if the reader is aware of the class connotations and the suggestion of snobbery.

This aspect of teaching English is summed up by Beck et al. in *Bringing Words to Life* (2013: 5):

> ... students must have the skills to infer word meaning information from the contexts they read. The problem is that many students in need of vocabulary development do not engage in wide reading, especially of the kinds of books that contain unfamiliar vocabulary, and these students are less able to derive meaningful information from the context.

So, progress is not just about reading more but reading texts with increased challenge. The point in the unit at which the pupils will be expected to choose link reading is going to vary, but it could be that the access strategies have opened up enough curiosity to offer it now.

These reading links explore a range of tones across a wide readability spread:

❧ 'The Beauty of It' by Don L. Lee

❧ 'My Shadow' by Robert Louis Stevenson

❧ *Anna Hibiscus* by Atinuke

❧ *The Wizard of Oz* by Frank L. Baum (Unit 14 in *Opening Doors to Quality Writing for Ages 6 to 9*)

❧ *The Fox and the Star* by Coralie Bickford-Smith

❧ *Pinocchio* by Carlo Collodi (Unit 13)

❧ *I Am Henry Finch* by Alexis Deacon and Viviane Schwarz

❧ *Pool* by JiHyeon Lee

- *Scout and the Sausage Thief* by Gill Lewis and Sarah Horne
- *Nothing to Be Afraid Of* by Jan Mark
- *Varjak Paw* by S. F. Said and Dave McKean
- *Amazing Grace* by Mary Hoffman and Caroline Binch

Reading journeys

It's time to read more from *Peter Pan*. Mrs Darling has put her family to bed and has nodded off to sleep.

While she slept she had a dream. She dreamt that the Neverland had come too near and that a strange boy had broken through from it. …

The dream by itself would have been a trifle, but while she was dreaming the window of the nursery blew open, and a boy did drop on the floor. He was accompanied by a strange light, no bigger than your fist, which darted about the room like a living thing; and I think it must have been this light that wakened Mrs Darling.

She started up with a cry, and saw the boy, and somehow she knew at once that he was Peter Pan … He was a lovely boy, clad in skeleton leaves and the juices that ooze out of trees; but the most entrancing thing about him was that he had all his first teeth. When he saw she was a grown-up, he gnashed the little pearls at her. …

Mrs Darling screamed, and, as if in answer to a bell, the door opened, and Nana entered, returned from her evening out. She growled and sprang at the boy, who leapt lightly through the window. Again Mrs Darling screamed, this time in distress for him, for she thought he was killed, and she ran down into the street to look for his little body, but it was not there; and she looked up, and in the black night she could see nothing but what she thought was a shooting star.

She returned to the nursery, and found Nana with something in her mouth, which proved to be the boy's shadow. As he leapt at the window Nana had closed it quickly, too late to catch him, but his shadow had not had time to get out; slam went the window and snapped it off. …

But unfortunately Mrs Darling could not leave it hanging out at the window; it looked so like the washing and lowered the whole tone of the house. She thought of showing it to Mr Darling, but he was totting up winter great-coats for John and Michael, with a wet towel round his head to keep his brain clear, and it seemed a shame to trouble him; besides, she knew exactly what he would say: 'It all comes of having a dog for a nurse.'

She decided to roll the shadow up and put it away carefully in a drawer, until a fitting opportunity came for telling her husband. Ah me!

As you have opened so many doors to appreciation and understanding in the access strategies, the next steps can be accelerated. Set an open question with **radial questions** as support. Your pupils can move on at an appropriate pace but with all of them sharing the same objective.

Support: What do you find funny or absurd in the passage? Why did you laugh?	**Support:** Find examples of tone changes through the whole passage.

How does J. M. Barrie introduce us to the story of *Peter Pan*?

Support: Write out in a table with two columns: (1) all the action in the passage and (2) all the humour. Instead of a table you could mark the passage with different colours for (1) and (2). Was any of the action funny too?	**Greater depth:** Compare the entrance of the main character with the way in which another protagonist from a fantasy story is introduced. What do you notice about the similarities or differences?

Excellent responses will:

Key concept: exploring tone

❦ Show how the tone is both funny and dramatic.

❦ Explore the narrative viewpoint via Mrs Darling and the way the scene is described through her.

Key concept: building drama

❦ List some of the ways in which the story includes high drama and the absurd:

   🍂 The description of Peter compared with his teeth.

   🍂 Nana as a protective dog but also a nurse with human qualities.

   🍂 Mrs Darling's anxiety about Peter compared with rolling up the shadow like a piece of clothing.

   🍂 The violent treatment of the shadow – perceived as an intruder prior to the rolling up.

Make sure to put your expectations for excellence at the top of your success criteria. If excellence is expected from all then we may start to get it. Aspects of spelling, punctuation and grammar are as important as ever, but always teach them in context.

We can achieve quality text to quality writing journeys by emphasising style much more and showing how spelling, punctuation and grammar are vital components of an effective text. For example, examine the wonderful phrase 'skeleton leaves'. There is an opportunity to teach about the use of adjectives and metaphors simultaneously. The spelling of 'gnashed' could be compared with 'gnaw', or a lesson on the spelling of adverbs like 'unfortunately' could be included. Your pupils will be asking so many questions about the shadow and the strange behaviour of Nana, about the strange light which seems alive and about Mrs Darling, that they will be listening more intently when you talk about spelling, punctuation and grammar. They will also be ready to develop that taster draft into some very exciting writing.

Wings to fly

Use titles which will help your pupils to experiment with storytelling and the use of a particular tone to define the narrative. They should excel at imitating J. M. Barrie or writing variations on themes from the passage. Make the link between reading and writing!

Try negotiating these possibilities:

- My Stolen Shadow (first-person practice)
- The Strange Light – which tells the story of the shadow trapped in the room
- Nana the Dog Nurse and Peter Pan – what happens next?
- Mrs Darling's Diary
- Peter Returns for the Shadow
- The Shadow Escapes from the Drawer
- Tinker Bell's Advice to Peter

These titles are open to extension, shortening or adapting. Work with your pupils to find the best possible writing route for them to enjoy the process.

Drama may provide even further access:

❦ Role play the movement of the shadow.

❦ Ask one pupil to be the 'strange light' and another to be Peter. Do they know who the light actually is?

❦ Bring the whole scene together to learn more about the way in which humour expressed via drama can help with an understanding of tone.

Once Upon a Time There Was a Piece of Wood

Pinocchio by Carlo Collodi

Opening Doors key strategy: crafting comedy

How does comedy help to shape the narrative of a famous story?

How successfully can you create an unusual fantasy character?

Access strategies

The popularity of *Pinocchio* endures, but it could be that you will be the first person to introduce this famous story to your pupils. A plethora of films, animations, adaptations and illustrated books have tended to leave in the imagination the image of a nose which lengthens when a lie is told, as well as a number of extraordinary adventures: being pursued by assassins, becoming a watchdog and Pinocchio finding his maker in the stomach of a dogfish! On rereading it, we found it quite extraordinary: a series of wonderfully absurd and frightening adventures experienced by a wooden puppet who is endlessly searching for moral guidance.

We think the beginning sets the tone and would recommend using it to teach your pupils how Collodi develops the language for an unlikely tale. It is part slapstick, part drama and very theatrical.

To open doors to new learning about comedy, initially tell your children nothing about *Pinocchio*, except that Master Cherry is chopping up wood and has heard a voice. Explore this extract:

He turned his terrified eyes all around the room to try and discover where the little voice could possibly have come from, but he saw nobody! He looked under the bench – nobody; he looked into a cupboard that was always shut – nobody; he looked into a basket of shavings and sawdust – nobody; he even opened the door of the shop and gave a glance into the street – and still nobody. Who, then, could it be?

'I see how it is,' he said, laughing and scratching his wig; 'evidently that little voice was all my imagination. Let us set to work again.'

And taking up the axe he struck a tremendous blow on the piece of wood.

'Oh! Oh! You have hurt me!' cried the same little voice dolefully.

In groups of three, ask the children to act out the drama to help them understand more about the ways in which threat and humour can work together: the first pupil should play the part of Master Cherry, the second should pretend to be a talking log and the third should take notes and give advice on the performance. The children should take turns being Master Cherry and try to improve each time. This is a variation on a learning triad exercise (where there is a talker, an interviewer and a note-taker) and gives scope for reflection and sharing ideas across the whole class.

The following questions should help the note-taker:

❧ Did they capture the fear of Master Cherry in his movements?

❧ Are they liable to make the audience laugh when they perform the routine to the whole group?

❧ What does 'dolefully' mean? How should the voice of the log come across?

If you are using this extract with younger pupils who are not used to taking notes, a simple table like the one that follows can help with observation and feedback. Visuals could be used as well as words, providing the feedback brings out comments which can lead to improvements in the performance and which make links with the meaning of the passage. What did your pupils notice?

Are the eyes 'terrified'?	
Are the movements effective?	
Does he scratch his head in a curious way?	

Was the axe brought down like it was in the text?	
Did the voice of the log sound sorrowful?	

A **taster draft** will follow naturally. Ask the children to use what has been learnt about comedic writing to compose the next paragraph. Will Master Cherry keep hitting the log? The draft could borrow Collodi's phrase as a title: 'Once Upon a Time There Was a Piece of Wood'.

Feedback should centre around how to develop the humour further. Give the children opportunities for different kinds of practice based on your advice:

❦ Did the writing develop the comic situation in clever ways?

❦ How effectively was the personality of the log presented?

❦ Was direct speech used well?

❦ Were more moments of absurd drama created?

Cognitive scientist Daniel T. Willingham makes much of the importance of practice: 'For a new skill to become automatic or for new knowledge to become long lasting, sustained practice *beyond the point of mastery* is necessary … Practice until you are perfect and you will be perfect only briefly. What's necessary is sustained practice' (2004; original emphasis).

Bob says ...

Taster drafts, which are recommended throughout the 'Opening Doors' series, provide a way to plan for sustained practice. However, I see standards raised the most when the practice is varied, ambitious and includes high quality feedback and advice from teachers on how to improve. If not, it is possible to practice ad infinitum, repeating the same shortcomings.

Consider the use of dashes associated with the word 'nobody' or the meaning and spelling of 'dolefully'. At this taster draft stage, the pupils are particularly engaged with a new challenge and eager to learn, so it is the perfect opportunity to explore word roots, etymology and spelling rules. Grammar matters, and grammar for meaning matters most! 'Dolefully' is an adverb and learning how it sums up precisely the way the log is hurting is the kind of teaching that will link knowledge with improved writing in the application stage.

Reading journeys

Read the full extract – dramatically – to your audience, who should by now be revelling in the content and the humour! An old carpenter, Master Antonio (also called Master Cherry because of his red nose) starts to chop up an old log, only to find that it speaks and tells him not to strike so hard.

He turned his terrified eyes all around the room to try and discover where the little voice could possibly have come from, but he saw nobody! He looked under the bench – nobody; he looked into a cupboard that was always shut – nobody; he looked into a basket of shavings and sawdust – nobody; he even opened the door of the shop and gave a glance into the street – and still nobody. Who, then, could it be?

'I see how it is,' he said, laughing and scratching his wig; 'evidently that little voice was all my imagination. Let us set to work again.'

And taking up the axe he struck a tremendous blow on the piece of wood.

'Oh! Oh! You have hurt me!' cried the same little voice dolefully.

This time Master Cherry was petrified. His eyes started out of his head with fright, his mouth remained open, and his tongue hung out almost to the end of his chin, like a mask on a fountain. As soon as he had recovered the use of his speech, he began to say, stuttering and trembling with fear: 'But where on earth can that little voice have come from that said Oh! Oh!? ... Here there is certainly not a living soul. Is it possible that this piece of wood can have learnt to cry and to lament like a child? I cannot believe it. This piece of wood, here it is; a log for fuel like all the others, and thrown on the fire it would about to suffice to boil a saucepan of beans ... How then? Can anyone be hidden inside it? If anyone is hidden inside, so much the worse for him. I will settle him at once.'

So saying, he seized the poor piece of wood and commenced beating it without mercy against the walls of the room.

Then he stopped to listen if he could hear any little voice lamenting. He waited two minutes – nothing; five minutes – nothing; ten minutes – still nothing! …

Putting the axe aside he took his plane, to plane and polish the bit of wood; but whilst he was running it up and down he heard the same little voice say, laughing: 'Have done! you are tickling me all over!'

This time poor Master Cherry fell down as if he had been struck by lightning. When he at last opened his eyes he found himself seated on the floor.

His face was quite changed, even the end of his nose, instead of being crimson, as it was nearly always, had become blue from fright.

Decide which pupils can attempt the top-class 'Opening Doors' question without support and which individuals need more prompts and discoveries provided by the radial layouts.

Support:

How is repetition used in the passage?

Support:

Can you visualise the action? Describe your favourite moments and how they are made vivid.

How is the threat of violence expressed?

How is the humour developed in the opening of *Pinocchio*?

Support:

How are Master Cherry's thoughts to himself described? How is it funny?

Which sections remind you of a pantomime or farce? Why?

Greater depth:

Can you write about the most absurd moments? Why did they seem original to you?

Can you imagine this scene on the stage? Which parts would be the hardest to act and why?

Excellent responses will:

Key concept: humour in a fantasy tale

❦ Explore, using examples, how humour is created via:

- ஃ Direct speech (e.g. 'tickling' gives the log a personality).
- ஃ Master Cherry's inner monologue.
- ஃ Absurd drama (e.g. the talking log, sudden threats of 'killing', the voice in the log, the wig, the changing colours of Master Cherry's nose). Think of anything ridiculous which, simultaneously, we start to believe and accept.

Browse the **link reading** list to engage with other types of humour and comedy. Lots of teachers admit that the breadth of their own reading has grown as a result of using 'Opening Doors' texts; this should be a natural offshoot of delivering lessons around quality texts. It happens to us as well, as we too became more motivated to find out about the origins of *Pinocchio* or the Theatre of the Absurd.

Pinocchio occasionally tips towards tragedy to force home the morality of good behaviour, so you will need to introduce certain episodes to the children very carefully, especially the scene where Pinocchio is hanged and nearly dies. It is also quite distressing when he turns into a donkey! Overall, black humour seems to win the day in terms of tone, and the story retains an entertaining edge which is very different from Hans Christian Andersen, for example.

Beyond the limit – link reading

❦ *Peter Pan* by J. M. Barrie (Unit 12)

❦ *Cautionary Verses* by Hilaire Belloc

❦ *That Rabbit Belongs to Emily Brown* by Cressida Cowell and Neal Layton

❦ *I Am Henry Finch* by Alexis Deacon and Viviane Schwarz

❦ *Who Let the Gods Out?* by Maz Evans

❦ *Toys in Space* by Mini Grey

❦ *Dogger* by Shirley Hughes

❦ *I Want My Hat Back* (and other 'Hat' series books) by Jon Klassen

❦ *Lost in the Toy Museum: An Adventure* by David Lucas

❦ 'Uncle David's Nonsensical Story About Giants and Fairies' by Catherine Sinclair (Unit 11 in *Opening Doors to Quality Writing for Ages 6 to 9*)

You could also share other readings from *Pinocchio* or explore with the children the 2005 edition illustrated by Roberto Innocenti. You may also like to look at more humour with an Italian origin, such as 'Punch and Judy'. Try the Victoria and Albert Museum site: www.vam.ac.uk. Look up *commedia dell'arte* to find out more about this early form of professional theatre in Italy.

Wings to fly

You may stimulate the best writing from the children by getting them to focus on beginnings, humour and inventing comic moments, rather than writing a long story. There is plenty of choice in the titles, as always, which should enable them to exploit what they have learnt so far. Above all, the writing should be absurd, clever and yet believable. That is a challenge!

- Once Upon a Time There Was a … (use an object, not a place or person).

- After reading some more of *Pinocchio*, develop a single short adventure for the puppet.

- Create a single short adventure for a female puppet who misbehaves. Give her a new name which still sounds Italian.

- In the story it is Geppetto, a poor woodcarver, who actually carves the piece of wood into a puppet who becomes Pinocchio. Imagine that he actually carves the wood into something else, and tell the story of what happens.

- Pinocchio takes a walk in the world of the twenty-first century and then writes his diary!

- In one chapter, Pinocchio falls asleep and his legs get burnt off in the fire. Invent an episode for Pinocchio in which something nasty happens, but make it so ridiculous that we can all laugh. Imagine Pinocchio is writing to tell Geppetto about the episode.

- Write about a talking log in a completely different setting.

❦ Watch the 1940 Walt Disney film and write about why you think changes were made to the plot and characters (e.g. Jiminy Cricket).

The origins of slapstick and the absurd have led to innovations in theatre and film, as well as in children's literature, so your pupils' work will be part of a great tradition in comedy. Celebrate, share and read the children's humorous episodes, scenes and stories. Now you can apply the most effective success criteria of all: is it making everyone laugh?

Whirlpools!

'The Island of the Nine Whirlpools' by Edith Nesbit

Opening Doors key strategy: plot plans

How does a writer introduce a story?

Can you write your own starter for a fairy tale and challenge your friend to continue it?

Access strategies

You are going to be teaching your pupils how to devise a plot which can be a variation on tales from any tradition or culture. The challenge is to set up a likely story which a friend can continue!

Try exploring some key characters and aspects of the plot in 'The Island of the Nine Whirlpools':

❦ A griffin

❦ A dragon

❦ A king

❦ A queen

❦ A princess

❦ The nine whirlpools

Use a **link jotter** to encourage the children to think through possible associations with titles, people or places. The example below explores the question: what do whirlpools mean to you? In this instance there are six links with whirlpools, with 'sucking down' in the centre.

Ask your pupils to devise the central phrase first and then work outwards. The link jotter helps to build vocabulary and will come in useful when developing a plot later on. It encourages the idea that our initial thoughts are just a beginning and that a cognitive field of ideas can emerge.

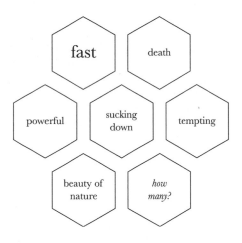

Ask the children to write a **taster draft** including vocabulary from the example, or from their own link jotter work, to craft a 100-word piece on the nature of a whirlpool. Unit 15 in *Opening Doors to Famous Poetry and Prose* features a short story by Edgar Allan Poe called 'A Descent into the Maelström' (maelström is an old Dutch word for whirlpool). Of course, your pupils could choose to write a taster draft on griffins, princesses or anything from the initial list. Feed back across the groups with advice based around the need for originality.

Now, let them know that the story has witches in it too!

A **continuum line** for a witch will start to sift and sort the children's expectations:

Totally evil
witch

Totally good
witch

Write down the name of a witch from any story on a sticky note. Ask the pupils where you should place it on the continuum line, once they have assessed the degree of good or evil. They must give their reasons for the positioning of the note! You can do a similar exercise for the dragon, griffin and so on. You may need to discover more about griffins first – they are half lion and half eagle and have their origins in Roman and Greek mythology. Writers adapt and play with past associations, so a powerful beast like the griffin becomes 'respectable' in Edith Nesbit's story – with a **tongue in cheek** reference to a good upbringing!

Make sure your pupils keep exploring patterns in their minds and creating new possibilities. This helps to stimulate ongoing ideas and is therefore at the heart of a richer curriculum. In *Tell Me*, Aidan Chambers (1991: 120) says: 'A great deal of critical activity, even of the most sophisticated kind, is concerned with finding patterns – of language, of narrative "codes", of plot, of images, of character, and the rest.'

Bob says ...

Patterns can only be accessed and articulated with the benefit of ongoing quality reading, so use the link reading list at any appropriate time and have the texts ready on the children's desks. The linking and sparking of ideas will become a habit for your pupils, and a world of language and stories will come alive. That is a gift for life!

Reading journeys

In 'The Island of the Nine Whirlpools', Edith Nesbit's wonderful variation on fairy tale themes and traditional tales, a king sent his queen to a witch to 'receive' a child – but he never expected to get a girl! The queen rewarded the 'ugly' witch with fifty kisses, being 'completely unaware that her husband, an 'enchanter', would not be best pleased. When the princess is 18 and shows spirit and loyalty to her mother, the king takes action.

Resource 48

And without another word he went off to his laboratory and worked all night, boiling different coloured things in crucibles, and copying charms in curious twisted letters from old brown books with mould stains on their yellowy pages.

The next day his plan was all arranged. He took the poor Princess to the Lone Tower, which stands on an island in the sea, a thousand miles from everywhere. He gave her a dowry, and settled a handsome income on her. He engaged a competent dragon to look after her, and also a respectable griffin whose birth and bringing-up he knew all about. And he said:

'Here you shall stay my dear, respectful daughter, till the clever man comes to marry you. He'll have to be clever enough to sail a ship through the Nine Whirlpools that spin round the island, and to kill the dragon and the griffin. Till he comes you'll never get any older or any wiser. No doubt he will soon come. You can employ yourself by embroidering your wedding gown. I wish you joy, my dutiful child.'

And his car, drawn by live thunderbolts (thunder travels very fast), rose in the air and disappeared, and the poor Princess was left, with the dragon and the griffin, in the Island of the Nine Whirlpools.

The Queen, left at home, cried for a day and a night, and then she remembered the witch and called to her. And the witch came, and the Queen told her all.

'For the sake of the twice twenty-five kisses you gave me,' said the witch, 'I will help you. But it is the last thing I can do, and it is not much. Your daughter is under a spell, and I can take you to her. But, if I do, you will have to be turned to stone, and to stay so till the spell is taken off the child.'

'I would be a stone for a thousand years,' said the poor Queen, 'if at the end of them I could see my Dear again.'

So, the plot is set up!

Use the suggested **radial questions** (see figure on page 215) in flexible ways. You could allocate questions to groups based on prior attainment or give them the chance to choose a question themselves. You may wish to teach in a more **direct transmission** mode to explain and model some of the concepts in the **excellent responses will** list. Use a **mini-plenary** to bring together ideas and find out where progress has faltered.

Excellent responses will:

Key concept: plot originality

- ❦ Refer to the initial images of the king as an evil wizard.

- ❦ Explore the words 'crucible' and 'dowry' and consider why the king mentions this when, in effect, he is imprisoning his daughter.

- ❦ Discuss the use of humour and irony to advance the plot – for example, what kind of tone is the king using when he says 'I wish you joy'?

Support:
How can the princess be rescued? What questions are set up which will be answered in the story?

Support:
How is the king's character portrayed? Think about the vocabulary and images associated with him.

Support:
Which words are used to describe the princess? Is there a pattern? Does it matter who uses the words?

How does Edith Nesbit give her readers the sense of a developing plot?

Support:
What kind of humour does Edith Nesbit include? Find some examples you like and explain why you like them.

Greater depth:
Can you describe the tone of the text? Are you expecting a serious, funny or tragic tale? How does the style of a story support the type of plot we expect? Can you compare the humour with Unit 13?

- ❦ Talk about how the dragon and the griffin are described.
- ❦ Consider how the subplot with the witch starts to give the reader ideas for predicting the climax of the story.

You can co-construct the success criteria having taught new ideas about plot, prediction and variation in fairy tales using this extract. As Claire Gadsby observes in *Perfect Assessment for Learning* (2012: 29–30), 'A few minutes spent really exploring the success criteria with learners could be the key difference in terms of learners making progress … try not to impose a ceiling or limit on what pupils can achieve.'

Beyond the limit – link reading

These texts will help to provide a more varied idea of plots in classic tales, past and present:

- ❦ 'The Frost, the Sun, and the Wind' by Charles Downing (Unit 9)
- ❦ 'Blackberry Blue' by Jamila Gavin (Unit 8)
- ❦ *Classic Fairy Tales* by Michael Foreman
- ❦ *One Thousand and One Arabian Nights* by Geraldine McCaughrean
- ❦ *Perseus* by Geraldine McCaughrean
- ❦ *Hansel and Gretel* by Michael Morpurgo and Emma Chichester Clark
- ❦ *Pattan's Pumpkin* by Chitra Soundar and Frane Lessac
- ❦ *You're Safe With Me* by Chitra Soundar and Poonam Mistry
- ❦ *Chalk Eagle* by Nazli Tahvili

❦ *Five Children and It* by Edith Nesbit (Unit 15 in *Opening Doors to Quality Writing for Ages 6 to 9*.

Edith Nesbit is best known for her children's stories like *The Railway Children* and *The Phoenix and the Carpet*. The full story of 'The Island of the Nine Whirlpools' can be found at: https://www.storyberries.com/the-island-of-the-nine-whirlpools/.

Wings to fly

Ask the children to learn from the plotline used by Edith Nesbit to set up their own story for a friend to read – and then continue. They could think about:

❦ The image of the king.

❦ The humour.

❦ The plot involving a princess who has been a bit too smart for her father's liking and the idea that someone 'clever' needs to rescue her.

❦ The idea of turning to stone (which features in Greek mythology – Medusa, for example).

❦ A very different kind of witch!

Younger pupils may prefer to write a beginning which features some of the characters from 'The Island of the Nine Whirlpools' or a book from the link reading list, rather than a full, sustained story. If so, ask them to write an introduction to entertain a friend or the whole class. It must make them want to continue reading it! We're sure some of them will.

Encourage the pupils to plan the whole plot so they have the big picture in their mind whilst they are writing. What will their plot line be? Could they write the blurb for the back cover before writing the story?

Bob says ...

If we find that a choice of routes or titles stimulates creativity, then why not teach and encourage a plethora of planning aids too! I always find that asking pupils to write a potential blurb for the back cover before they have written the story forces them to think about the whole shape of the plot.

Who can write the tale with the best plot? A whole-class storytelling session will be appreciated by the children, particularly if you also include tips and advice. A chosen few could be read out during assembly or posted on the school website.

Bob says ...

Different kinds of concept maps or story mountains could be used to encourage planning beyond the standard beginning, middle and end. Shapes that have worked for me include rivers showing subplots as meanders, main episodes drawn in detail or the ending planned first at the apex of a triangle.

A discussion of gender bias will come up quite naturally as you explain the task. It is vital to raise and discuss relevant questions:

❦ Is there a pattern in well-known fairy tales concerning the behaviour of males and females or kings and queens? What about princesses?

❦ Do the covers of the books in your library suggest any kind of presumption about books for 'typical' boys or girls? Is there such a thing?

❦ How was Hans Christian Andersen's 'The Snow Queen' adapted in the film *Frozen*? How were males and females represented?

Some pupils will be ready to explore further, create an anthology or craft more variations on this theme, so here are a few more possibilities:

❦ Use the end of the story as a stimulus:

I have no doubt that you will wish to know what the Princess lived on during the long years when the dragon did the cooking. My dear, she lived on her income – and that is a thing that a great many people would like to be able to do.

❦ Write your own continuation to 'The Island of the Nine Whirlpools' with the dragon playing a leading role.

❦ Turned to Stone

❦ The Griffin with Attitude

I love this quote from the preface to C. S. Lewis' *The Lion, the Witch and the Wardrobe*, in which he sums up the enduring value and appeal of fairy tales for us all: 'some day you will be old enough to start reading fairy tales again'.

The Butterfly Dance

The Story of the Blue Planet
by Andri Snær Magnason

Opening Doors key strategy: scene setter

Can you understand how an author creates a distinct setting?

How well can you write about your setting – one full of wonders?

Access strategies

Ask the children to look at the illustration:

- What is the 'mood' of the picture? How do you know?
- What puzzles you?
- Can you say what kind of music might accompany the illustration?

A **music moment** may deepen the pupils' thinking, so find out if any of these possibilities fit with their idea of butterflies in a cave:

🦋 'Butterfly' by the nineteenth century Norwegian composer Edvard Grieg.

🦋 The 'Lever du Jour' (sunrise) sequence from Maurice Ravel's 1912 ballet *Daphnis et Chloé*.

The key strategy in this unit is 'scene setter', so you may wish to utilise the **link reading** texts at an early stage. We have included picture books as a matter of course, because high level visual literacy can be developed by using challenging questions and introducing comparative concepts. If you can teach your pupils about scenes of wonder at the access stage, it will boost their ability to understand the full extract and, eventually, the whole of *The Story of the Blue Planet*. Ask your pupils which scene of wonder they respond to best in the books which link with the objectives. Ask them to list what kinds of settings they might expect in a scene of wonder.

For your own deepening understanding of the rationale and terminology behind the potential of picture books as quality texts, we would highly recommend *Developing Children's Critical Thinking Through Picturebooks* by Mary Roche. She succinctly sums up in a tweet the richness of picture books in the curriculum: '[Picture books], especially wordless ones, are complex, intriguing & demand high comprehension & visual literacy skills. Such [books] do not yield up meaning easily' (@marygtroche, 30 July 2018).

An early **taster draft** now may play with the ideas already discussed. Ask the children to write a paragraph describing the scene they see with the aim of creating a special atmosphere for their setting. A

mood barometer may help your pupils to gauge what kind of atmosphere they need to devise.

```
dark,
menacing
```

```
pleasant
with hints
of danger
```

```
light,
positive
feel
```

Words, phrases or pictures could be added in the white space to plan out the taster draft, but it is simply a guide. The draft should not only be factually descriptive, it must also develop the atmosphere. That is more challenging! As part of some learning dialogues with your class, try to model how atmosphere and mood can vary depending on the writer's intentions. Authors can play with readers' responses by establishing a mood which then subtly changes. The possibilities are endless, which is why reading lots of texts is vital.

The link reading could be introduced before the taster draft to broaden the pupils' notions of setting and mood. You could take the opportunity to suggest that there might be some hidden meaning which is implied by the mood of the setting.

Bob says ...

Much thought goes into teaching inference in a text – but don't forget to offer your pupils opportunities to practise inference in their own writing too.

Feed your pupils a sliver of text so they can compare their own draft with Andri Snær Magnason's:

As the light flooded the cave and shone on their wings, something wonderful happened: the butterflies awoke from their sleep. Very slowly and calmly they moved their wings and then rose in the air, one by one, and flew out of the mouth of the cave. They followed the sun for a whole day, circling the planet over land and sea, mountains and valleys, before fluttering back into the cave and falling asleep again, not to awaken until another year had passed.

The 'Opening Doors' question sets up deeper thinking and often includes prompts and scaffolds to support routes to mastering the **key concepts**. Try plunging in with this challenge:

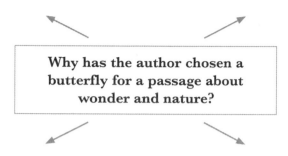

Why has the author chosen a butterfly for a passage about wonder and nature?

Your pupils can use highlighter pens to search for evidence of the theme of wonder. Encourage them to highlight a word or phrase, discuss it in a group and then share it with the whole class – **mark and note**. You can transfer and apply this technique to most texts as it gives the children practice in understanding the concept behind the work. Highlighting parts of speech can come next. In this way, the pupils are not just identifying a verb, for example, for its own sake, but learning why it has been used and how successful it is.

You will get some fascinating responses. The best ones will call on prior personal associations with butterflies as well as nature programmes. General knowledge is much underrated; the enriched learning going on every day in every aspect of a child's life is often the context in which questions and answers are found and problems solved.

Some of the following ideas may come up:

❦ Is a butterfly a fragile, coloured beauty?

❦ Is every butterfly different?

❦ Can we capture and hold a butterfly?

❦ What is the lifespan of a butterfly?

❦ Are butterflies always beautiful?

❦ Do we value beauty above other things?

Don't forget the role of philosophy in a richer English curriculum. Many schools using 'Opening Doors' have reported greatly enhanced opportunities for debating, challenging and enquiring. You can find out more about Philosophy for Children at: www.sapere.org.uk.

What are your pupils' conclusions about the wider meaning of the butterfly? You might want to teach them more about the use of symbols and link this with Unit 9 on 'The Frost, the Sun, and the Wind'.

Reading journeys

Magnason's *The Story of the Blue Planet* has become a modern classic because of its environmental themes and creative, humorous style. The children on the blue planet seem eternally happy until the arrival of Gleesome Goodday and promises of a more exciting way of life and the ability to fly across the sky. Just what is Goodday trying to sell and what does he want in return? The book would be an apt selection for a class reader, but first collect responses to your reading of the following extract, which gives a little more context to the strategic butterfly passage.

The blue planet is inhabited by children who never grow old. They eat when they are hungry and sleep when they are tired.

The children had endless adventures on the blue planet. They could follow fireflies in the dark or climb rocky cliffs and jump into warm waters. They could gather shells on the beach and watch the sea turtles crawl ashore to lay their eggs. There were high cliffs full of nesting birds and cold white glaciers that crawled to the sea, crunching and crumbling. The forests were light-green during the day when the tigers and parrots were about, but they turned dark-green in the evening when the wolves began howling, and black-green at night when the bats awoke and spiders with hairy legs wove their webs between branches.

Once a year an incredible event took place on the blue planet. A ray of light would burst through a little hole in the wall of a cave in the Blue Mountains. This was no ordinary cave. It was full of sleeping butterflies.

As the light flooded the cave and shone on their wings, something wonderful happened: the butterflies awoke from their sleep. Very slowly and calmly they moved their wings and then rose in the air, one by one, and flew out of the mouth of the cave. They followed the sun for a whole day, circling the planet over land and sea, mountains and valleys, before fluttering back into the cave and falling asleep again, not to awaken until another year had passed.

The flight of the butterflies was the greatest wonder on the blue planet and a day of true happiness. The children would lie on their backs and watch the butterflies fill the sky until they disappeared with the sun beyond the horizon.

Some pupils will be able to answer the main 'Opening Doors' question, whilst others may need to tackle the support questions first.

Support:
List the ways in which the first paragraph creates a feeling of joy. How is this done? How is this completed in the third paragraph?

Support:
What does 'endless adventures' mean? What would your endless adventures be if you had the choice?

Explore the many ways in which the author sets up a scene of beauty and wonder.

Support:
Collect verbs associated with the butterflies, like 'fluttered'. How does each verb tell us something different but also link with the others?

Greater depth:
Write about all the references to light in the passage. List them and then find any patterns of meaning. What does light symbolise? What does 'fill the sky' mean? Is there an imaginative interpretation?

The support questions don't have to be set like exercises but can be part of a range of **dialogic talk**. This could include:

❦ Debates about the environment and our place within it.

❦ Philosophical communities of enquiry on whether your class would like to live forever or play all day.

❦ Exploring the meaning and interpretation of fascinating words – for example, everyone writing down a definition for 'wonder' and then comparing them around the class.

❦ Setting regular challenges about meaning and metaphor – for example, ask your class if the writer is describing a kind of Eden? Where does the word 'Eden' originate?

Some people worry about children being encouraged to talk when they might not have the knowledge to do it well. But surely the development of all skills and knowledge is a work in progress, for adults as well as children. The earlier productive talk begins, the more confidence can grow. If we wait until we are all 'experts' on a subject before we can speak up, we will be in for a long wait.

Your pupils' oracy skills can grow through exploring a beautiful piece of writing like *The Story of the Blue Planet*. The fantasy paradise will stimulate new learning based around familiar images, like those of the butterfly, whilst the concepts in the story will stimulate fresh delight and curiosity.

Research by the Education Endowment Foundation has found evidence that dialogic talk can lead to gains for pupils in language, mathematics and science.

You can read a summary of the findings at: https://educationendowmentfoundation.org.uk/projects-and-evaluation/projects/dialogic-teaching.

Excellent responses will:

Key concept: scene setting

- Explain, with examples, how a kind of paradise is described:
  - The use of verbs.
  - The creation of a pattern of 'endless adventures'.
  - The use of light and colours.

Key concept: symbols

- Explore the butterfly images.
- Describe the structure of the sentences:
  - The use of summary or topic sentences.
  - The use of shorter sentences.

Beyond the limit – link reading

On the theme of living forever:

- *Tuck Everlasting* by Natalie Babbitt
- *How to Live Forever* by Colin Thompson

Picture books with wondrous scene setting:

❦ *Belonging* by Jeannie Baker

❦ *The Fox and the Star* by Coralie Bickford-Smith

❦ *What's Under the Bed?* by Mick Manning and Brita Granström

❦ *Greenling* by Levi Pinfold

❦ *You're Safe With Me* by Chitra Soundar and Poonam Mistry

❦ *Chalk Eagle* by Nazli Tahvili

❦ *The Sand Horse* by Ann Turnbull

❦ *The Tin Forest* by Helen Ward and Wayne Anderson

❦ *Free Fall* by David Wiesner

❦ *Teacup* by Rebecca Young and Matt Ottley

Wings to fly

Return to the taster drafts. Ask your pupils to consider the advice given on scene setting and develop some more sustained writing on one of these themes. Be explicit about what has been learnt from Magnason's writing and encourage them to apply some of the strategies discussed. It might be:

❦ Creating a distinct atmosphere and being consistent.

❦ Describing a scene but implying meaning between the lines.

❦ Using symbols or big picture motifs.

❦ Developing a particular narrative viewpoint.

Bob says ...

Relative success with all these subtle and sophisticated tools may be partly dependent on prior experiences, but aiming for excellence is for all learners.

Other possibilities include:

- ❦ Write about very different 'endless adventures' on a fantasy planet.

- ❦ As the light flooded the cave and shone on their wings, something wonderful happened …

- ❦ Write about something suitable that happens next but not with reference to butterflies.

- ❦ In the book, an adult, Gleesome Goodday, arrives and everything changes. Invent your own adult who invades the beautiful environment of the blue planet.

- ❦ This Was No Ordinary Cave

- ❦ The Red Planet: An Introduction

- ❦ The City of Peace at Midnight

- ❦ Ten Hours Without Adults

- ❦ The Advantages of Being Young Forever

We've referred to *The Story of the Blue Planet* as a modern classic, but all such labels are open to discussion. It takes the passing of time and the passing on of a book from generation to generation for the 'classic' billing to stick universally. One thing is for sure: many of the picture books and children's fiction of today are of a very high quality, so which ones do you think will be read in a hundred years' time? The 'Opening Doors' series has often focused on providing challenging texts from the past to enable deeper opportunities for learning, but in the best primary classrooms, past and present literature coexist to enthral the young readers and writers of today.

Glossary

Assonance

When writers use vowel sounds repeated for effect it is called assonance. Sometimes this is seen in clever rhyming.

Bookends approach

Beginnings and endings can be offered to support access to meaning. Explorations around the language can stimulate **taster drafts**, questions and a lot of fun!

Calligrams

Texts set out so that their visualisation forms an image linked with the content or theme of the text. They are also referred to as shape poems.

Choose and change

A quick way of remembering that every word counts. Use regular exercises to show that synonyms may have similar meanings but they are not the same. Make sure your pupils are aware of the critical decisions that writers make about word usage.

Continuum line

Once you have set two ends of a continuum, the pupils can decide which words or ideas belong at which position along the line. Discourage rapid decision-making based on 'right' or 'wrong' and instead encourage reflection and the weighing of ideas using evidence. You might say to your pupils, 'To what extent do you think ...?' You could first debate a position as a class and then ask the children to stand along a continuum line at the front of the classroom. Explore the issue or idea further and then see who has adjusted their position.

Deep objective

We refer to this as a way of signalling the need for an objective which genuinely sets up depth and challenge. We usually phrase this as a question.

Dialogic talk

In a dialogic classroom, the teacher and pupils work on the belief that knowledge and understanding are built through discourse. Teachers cannot assume that learners have the necessary oracy skills to explore ideas purposefully together through talk, but they can build such skills with their learners over time through practice and reflection. For more information see: https://www.educ.cam.ac.uk/research/groups/cedir/ or https://www.robinalexander.org.uk/dialogic-teaching/.

Didactic teaching

This phrase has been used for a long time to suggest teacher instruction. On those occasions when new knowledge needs to be explained and pupils guided very definitely, a didactic method can be employed with success. Outstanding teachers know how to adapt their style and choose the right methodology for the right objective.

Direct transmission

Teaching as transmission is the act of transferring facts and concepts from teacher to pupil. The new learning then has to be replicated in some way to 'prove' that the new body of knowledge has been understood and stored in the memory. Direct transmission can be useful in short bursts when you need to explain something in detail, particularly if it needs to be modelled. Some schools use this method frequently and others don't like it at all. We are constantly advising teachers to be flexible and to find the right methodology to fit a particular objective or need.

Excellent responses will (include)

This is a suggested way of ensuring that the most ambitious criteria for success are presented up front. It supports classroom discussions about how the most ambitious challenges can be achieved.

Hardest question first

This represents a reversal from the traditional method of moving from easy to very hard in a linear way. It can be very revealing and surprising, but it must be accompanied by support strategies so that approaches can be personalised according to progress. It is always important to plan from the top to include able learners but there are knock-on benefits for all the class. It does not mean that basic comprehension questions are not needed, but it does encourage us to ask questions about when we set them and for whom.

Imperative

A command which can take many forms. Imperatives help authors to add urgency to their writing.

Key concepts

One way of designing a richer English curriculum is to map out key concepts for each objective to ensure continuity and progression year by year. This tends to support challenging thinking for all because a concept must be mastered; the chosen text provides the means to explore the objectives fully. The resulting knowledge and skills can then be applied in more challenging contexts. A concept may be revisited and applied to progressively harder texts throughout Key Stages 1–4, with deeper knowledge and skills built in each time.

Link jotter

A technique which involves using hexagons to explore vocabulary and meaning in a fun and enjoyable way, but which also encourages children to make connections.

Link reading

Try to cross-reference books and poems that you expect your pupils to read. This prevents wider reading from being regarded as an optional or discrete part of the curriculum. Ensure that link reading is mapped in as part of continuity and progression.

Lyric poem

The lyric poem derives from Ancient Greek literature. Originally, a performance would have been accompanied by a stringed instrument called a lyre – hence lyric. A lyric poem will have a strong melodic quality, often achieved through rhythm, rhyme or other sound effects. It expresses personal feeling or emotions and is typically written in the first person.

Mark and note

A way of retaining the relationship a pupil develops with the text by marking parts of speech or noticeable features, but with more emphasis on asking questions about them. Pupils should explain why they have highlighted certain passages of text and share their views. This also gives the teacher a chance to intervene and clarify any learning points.

Metre

Metre is a unit of verse which can be used in many different combinations. See http://www.poetryarchive.org/glossary/metre for a brief guide.

Mini-plenary

These are feedback sessions with huge opportunities for learning. There should be the chance to share, question and explore progress. You can also teach explicit aspects of spelling, punctuation and grammar in context. Deeper learning and improved outcomes can then follow. Suggested questions might be: what have you found hard? What has interested you the most? How can you improve your writing? What progress have you made?

Modelling

Teacher modelling of a skill is powerful when it is metacognitive. This means working through a response to a text, question or composition and sharing not just your choices but also how you got there: the process and the struggle. This opens up the dialogic process for learners. Moving from 'I' to 'we' to 'you' is key when modelling to encourage learners to make the process their own.

Monitoring question

Good readers have a constant dialogue in their heads as they read. They monitor not just for literal sense but also for reader response: 'Am I starting to think differently about these characters? Are things getting a little worrying here? Goodness! I never thought that would happen!' Giving your class a monitoring question upfront to help focus their inner dialogue makes the reading process overt and visible for those still being inducted into the thinking habits of a reader.

Mood barometer

A way of explicitly planning out how a mood setting might be developed or whether there might need to be a change of mood. It is a simple planning aid, but it makes pupils think harder about their writing when creating atmospheres and settings.

Music moments

These are advised throughout the 'Opening Doors' series and are about much more than background music. Music moments can act like the soundtrack to a film – reinforcing meaning and supporting poetry or prose as a performance.

Onomatopoeia

Onomatopoeic words give expression and life to sounds – for example, the 'rustle' of autumn leaves. Try to get your pupils to use onomatopoeia more in their writing, rather than just identifying it as a figure of speech.

Personification

The figurative attribution of human characteristics to something inanimate or non-human.

Quadrant boxes

There are numerous variations on quadrants which encourage linking, comparing and evaluating. Aidan Chambers (1991) emphasises the importance of many kinds of connections.

Radial questions

Instead of setting out questions in a traditional linear way, why not offer possibilities radiating outwards from a central, high level question? This gives you the chance to personalise support and introduce new challenges as appropriate. It is a flexible strategy and encourages the pupils to focus on the quality answers needed.

Reading forum

The classroom can be the perfect place to test out readers' responses to a writer's emerging work – if the teacher builds and models a safe space for honest, focused responses to be shared with the writer. It provides a concrete way to test the writer's intent: what does this writing make us think and feel? Writer, is this what you had hoped for? If not, what might you need to change? If yes, what choices built that response?

Reading journey

Instead of using the term 'comprehension', why not talk about reading journeys? Emphasise that active and independent approaches to reading make understanding harder texts exciting and full of enquiry – a reading journey for life!

River of connections

Rivers are often used metaphorically to illustrate a journey, so we can use the river as a way of exploring increasingly complex links and associations with chosen words, with the simpler ones at the source and the more complex ones at the mouth.

Semantic field

A set of words that are related to each other through their meaning. As a group, they can build a tone or mood, or even encourage an emotional response from the reader.

Sequencing

Sequencing is a popular way of cutting up a text into sections and then asking pupils to reassemble it in the correct order. When combined with apt teacher interventions and advice, it can support meaning-making in very effective ways, including an understanding of punctuation usage.

SOLO taxonomy

The structure of observed learning outcomes (SOLO) taxonomy is widely used in schools, particularly to support mastery learning. Devised by John Biggs and Kevin Collis, it supports the development of understanding through a unit of learning. For more information visit: www.johnbiggs. com.au/academic/solo-taxonomy.

Syncopation

In music, syncopation involves disrupting the listener's expectations by stressing weak beats. We like to think that when reading different versions of fairy tales, readers can hear how writers are riffing on familiar story patterns by drawing attention to unexpected elements and disturbing the usual flow of the narrative.

Synonym continuum

Synonyms are different words with the same meaning. The mongrel nature of the English language means that we can often choose from a wide bank of words that have similar meanings which have entered the language from different word routes. Just think of the difference between kill, murder and assassinate, and how differently we respond to those words. To build a mental model of how writers might make vocabulary choices, you can build a synonym continuum – like a washing line – that moves from formal to informal choices, from emotive to neutral, from serious to comic, from epic to domestic. There are not good or bad words; there are only choices and their consequences.

Taster draft

The access strategies should include an early chance to write. This kind of draft should be enriching, not laborious. Your young writers can experiment with style and get advice from you at the point of the most intense enjoyment and deepest learning. The taster draft is a powerful learning vehicle for the improved full version they will write later on.

Think, pair, share

All pupils reflect in silence on a challenging question, then share their thoughts with a talking partner. In this way, participation can be expected from all in a whole-class debate.

Tongue in cheek

This idiom refers to a humorous statement made in a mocking kind of way, although a serious point is often being made.

White space thinking

This is a very common but effective strategy for encouraging pupils to write notes and questions in the spaces around texts, rather than being limited to answers in boxes.

Word construction

We can build words in English through strings of sound – hence phonics. But the world of related vocabulary opens up to learners when they see that we also build words through bricks of meaning that we call morphemes: not just play but playful, playing, replay. It is the key to unlocking spelling and vocabulary growth.

Zoom closer

Using the language of media studies can be very useful. Just as a camera zooms in, so too can the teacher offer a magnified view of a particular image or concept by focusing on part of the text. A visualiser can quite literally 'zoom in' on the subject.

Bibliography

Primary sources

Agard, John (1988). 'Poetry Jump-Up', in Grace Nichols (ed.), *Poetry Jump-Up: A Collection of Black Poetry*. London: Puffin.

Agard, John (2017a). 'An Off-the-Record Conversation', in *The Rainmaker Danced*. London: Hodder.

Agard, John (2017b). 'When Questions Are Bliss', in *The Rainmaker Danced*. London: Hodder.

Agard, John and Nichols, Grace (eds) (1996). *A Caribbean Dozen*. London: Walker Books.

Andersen, Hans Christian (2002 [1845]). *The Little Match Girl*. Bristol: Pook Press.

Anderson, Sophie (2018). *The House with Chicken Legs*. London: Usborne.

Atinuke (2007). *Anna Hibiscus*. London: Walker.

Babbitt, Natalie (2003 [1975]). *Tuck Everlasting*. London: Bloomsbury.

Baker, Jeannie (2004). *Belonging*. London: Walker Books.

Barrie, James Matthew (1994 [1911]). *Peter Pan*. Bristol: Parragon.

Baum, L. Frank (1993 [1900]). *The Wizard of Oz*. Ware: Wordsworth Classics.

Beecher, Catherine E. and Beecher Stowe, Harriet (1869). *The American Woman's Home*. Available at: http://www.gutenberg.org/ebooks/6598.

Belloc, Hilaire (1907 [1997]). *Cautionary Verses*. London: Children's Classics.

Bickford-Smith, Coralie (2015). *The Fox and the Star*. London: Random House.

Bloom, Valerie (2000a). 'Autumn Gilt', in *Let Me Touch the Sky: Selected Poems for Children*. London: Macmillan.

Bloom, Valerie (2000b). 'Tall Tales', in *Let Me Touch the Sky: Selected Poems for Children*. London: Macmillan.

Bloom, Valerie (2002). 'Next Door's Cat', in *Hot Like Fire and Other Poems*. London: Bloomsbury.

Blyton, Enid (2014 [1937]). *The Adventures of the Wishing-Chair*. London: Egmont.

Brand, Dionne (2006 [1979]). 'Wind', in *Earth Magic*. Toronto: Kids Can Press Ltd.

Brontë, Anne (2014 [1846]). 'Lines Composed in a Wood on a Windy Day', in *Poems by Currer, Ellis and Acton Bell*. N.p.: CreateSpace.

Browne, Frances (2007 [1857]). *Granny's Wonderful Chair*. Chapel Hill, NC: Yesterday's Classics.

Carter, James (2009). 'Gorilla Gazing', in James Carter and Graham Denton (eds), *Wild! Rhymes That Roar*. London: Macmillan.

Carroll, Lewis (1993 [1865]). *Alice's Adventures in Wonderland*. Ware: Wordsworth Classics.

Clare, John (2004 [1831]). 'The Hail Storm in June, 1831', in *Selected Poetry of John Clare*. London: Faber & Faber.

Clare, John (2012 [1827]). 'Pleasant Sounds', in Carol Ann Duffy (ed.), *101 Poems for Children: A Laureate's Choice*. London: Macmillan.

Clare, John (2017 [1837]). 'The Mouse's Nest', in Allie Esiri (ed.), *A Poem for Every Night of the Year*. London: Macmillan.

Coe, Mandy (2010). 'Extinct', in *If You Could See Laughter*. London: Salt.

Coelho, Joseph (2016a). 'The Watchers', in *Overheard in a Tower Block*. Hereford: Otter-Barry Books.

Coelho, Joseph (2016b). 'Welly', in *Overheard in a Tower Block*. Hereford: Otter-Barry Books.

Coelho, Joseph (2016c). 'Wind', in *Overheard in a Tower Block*. Hereford: Otter-Barry Books.

Coleridge, Samuel Taylor and Wordsworth, William (2006 [1797]). *Lyrical Ballads*. London: Penguin Classics.

Collodi, Carlo (1995 [1883]). *Pinocchio*. Ware: Wordsworth Editions.

Collodi, Carlo (2005 [1883]). *Pinocchio*, ill. Roberto Innocenti. London: Jonathan Cape.

Cornford, Frances (2013). 'The Night Express', in Carol Ann Duffy (ed.), *101 Poems for Children: A Laureate's Choice*, London: Macmillan.

Cowell, Cressida (2007). *That Rabbit Belongs to Emily Brown*, ill. Neal Layton. London: Orchard Books.

Crebbin, June (2006). 'Butterfly', in Pie Corbett (ed.), *The Works Key Stage 2*. London: Macmillan.

Creech, Sharon (2004). 'Footfalls', in *Heartbeat*. London: Bloomsbury.

Cummings, Edward Estlin (2012 [1923]). 'In Just-', in Carol Ann Duffy (ed.), *101 Poems for Children: A Laureate's Choice*. London: Macmillan.

Davies, William Henry (1911). 'Leisure', in *Songs of Joy and Others*. New York: University of California Libraries.

Davies, William Henry (2015 [1908]). *The Autobiography of a Super-Tramp*. London: Forgotten Books.

Deacon, Alexis (2014). *I Am Henry Finch*, ill. Viviane Schwarz. London: Walker Books.

de la Mare, Walter [1941]). 'The Wind', in *Bells and Grass*. London: Faber & Faber.

Dharker, Imtiaz (2012 [2006]). 'How to Cut a Pomegranate', in Carol Ann Duffy (ed.), *101 Poems for Children: A Laureate's Choice*. London: Macmillan.

Dickens, Charles (2000 [1839]). *Oliver Twist*. Ware: Wordsworth Classics.

Dickens, Charles (2004 [1861]). *Great Expectations*. London: Penguin.

Dickinson, Emily (2018 [1860]). 'Dear March – Come In –', in Susannah Herbert (ed.), *Poetry for a Change*. Hereford: Otter-Barry Books.

Downing Charles (1956a). *Russian Tales and Legends*. London: Oxford University Press.

Downing, Charles (1956b). 'The Frost, the Sun, and the Wind', in *Russian Tales and Legends*. London: Oxford University Press.

Duffy, Carol Ann (2007a). 'The Fruits, the Vegetables, the Flowers and the Trees', in *The Hat*. London: Faber & Faber.

Duffy, Carol Ann (2007b). 'I Adore Year 3', in *The Hat*. London: Faber & Faber.

Duffy, Carol Ann (2007c). 'The Look', in *The Hat*. London: Faber & Faber.

Eliot, Thomas Stearns (2010 [1939]). 'The Song of the Jellicles', in *Old Possum's Book of Practical Cats*. London: Faber & Faber.

Evans, Maz (2017). *Who Let the Gods Out?* Frome: Chicken House.

Farjeon, Eleanor (1958). 'Cat!', in *Silver, Sand and Snow*. London: Michael Joseph.

Farjeon, Eleanor (1996 [1957]). *Cats Sleep Anywhere*. London: Frances Lincoln.

Fogliano, Julie (2018). *A House That Once Was*, ill. Lane Smith. London: Roaring Book Press.

Foreman, Michael (2005). *Classic Fairy Tales*. New York: Sterling.

Forster, Edward Morgan (2000 [1910]). *Howards End*. London: Penguin.

French, Vivian (2015). *Yucky Worms*, ill. Jessica Ahlberg. London: Walker.

Frost, Robert (2009 [1915]). 'To the Thawing Wind', in *A Boy's Will*. London: Akasha Classics.

Frost, Robert (2013 [1923]). 'Stopping by Woods on a Snowy Evening', in *Collected Poems*. London: Vintage Classics.

Fusek Peters, Andrew (2009 [2001]). 'Attack of the Mutant Mangos: A Fruit Salad Ballad of Baddies', in Michael Rosen (ed.), *A–Z: The Best Children's Poetry from Agard to Zephaniah*. London: Penguin.

Gaiman, Neil (2017). *Norse Mythology*. New York: Norton.

Garlick, Raymond (2004). 'Alys at the Zoo', in *Fifty Strong: Fifty Poems Chosen by Teenagers for Teenagers*. Oxford: Heinemann.

Gavin, Jamila (2014a). *Blackberry Blue and Other Fairy Tales*. London: Random House.

Gavin, Jamila (2014b). 'Blackberry Blue', in *Blackberry Blue and Other Fairy Tales*. London: Random House.

Gavin, Jamila (2014c). 'The Night Princess', in *Blackberry Blue and Other Fairy Tales*. London: Random House.

Gittins, Chrissie (2010). 'Wasp on the Tube', in *The Humpback's Wail*. London: Rabbit Hole Publications.

Greenfield, Eloise (2018). *Thinker: My Puppy Poet and Me*, ill. Ehsan Abdollahi. London: Tiny Owl.

Grey, Mini (2013). *Toys in Space*. London: Red Fox.

Grimm, Jacob and Grimm, Wilhelm (2014). 'The Foundling', in *The Original Folk and Fairy Tales of the Brothers Grimm: The Complete First Edition*, tr. Jack Zipes. Princeton, NJ: Princeton University Press.

Hallworth, Grace (1990). *Cric Crac: A Collection of West Indian Stories*. London: Heinemann.

Hardy-Dawson, Sue (2017). 'November', in *Where Zebras Go*. Hereford: Otter-Barry Books.

Herbert, George (2007 [1633]). 'Easter Wings', in *The English Poems of George*

Herbert. Cambridge: Cambridge University Press.

Hodgson Burnett, Frances (2007 [1911]). *The Secret Garden*. Oxford: Oxford Children's Classics.

Hoffman, Mary (1991). *Amazing Grace*, ill. Caroline Binch. London: Frances Lincoln.

Hughes, Shirley (1977). *Dogger*. London: Red Fox.

Hughes, Ted (2008a). 'Snail', in *Collected Poems for Children*. London: Faber & Faber.

Hughes, Ted (2008b). 'Worm', in *Collected Poems for Children*. London: Faber & Faber.

Hutchins, Pat (2009 [1974]). *The Wind Blew*. London: Simon & Schuster.

Jacobs, Joseph (2015). *Indian Fairy Tales*. N.p.: CreateSpace.

Keane, Shake (1988). 'Once the Wind', in Grace Nichols (ed.), *Poetry Jump-Up: A Collection of Black Poetry*. London: Puffin.

Kipling, Rudyard (1994 [1932]). 'Four Feet', in *Collected Poems of Rudyard Kipling*. Ware: Wordsworth Editions.

Kipling, Rudyard (2013 [1894]). *The Jungle Books*. London: Penguin.

Klassen, Jon (2012). *I Want My Hat Back*. London: Walker Books.

Lear, Edward (2012 [1871]). 'The Owl and the Pussycat', in *The Owl and the Pussycat and Other Nonsense*. Dorking: Templar Publishing.

Lee, Don L. (1988). 'The Beauty of It', in Grace Nichols (ed.), *Poetry Jump-Up: A Collection of Black Poetry*. London: Puffin.

Lee, JiHyeon (2015). *Pool*. San Francisco, CA: Chronicle.

Lewis, Clive Staples (2009 [1950]). *The Lion, the Witch and the Wardrobe* (The Chronicles of Narnia). London: HarperCollins Children's Books.

Lewis, Clive Staples (2009 [1953]). *The Silver Chair* (The Chronicles of Narnia). London: HarperCollins Children's Books.

Lewis, Gill (2015). *Scout and the Sausage Thief*, ill. Sarah Horne. Oxford: Oxford University Press.

Lowbury, Edward (1990a [1972]). 'Prince Kano', in *Selected and New Poems, 1935–1989*. Frome: Hippopotamus.

Lowbury, Edward (1990b [1972]). 'The Storm', in *Selected and New Poems, 1935–1989*. Frome: Hippopotamus.

Lowbury, Edward (1990c [1972]). 'Unsecret', in *Selected and New Poems, 1935–1989*. Frome: Hippopotamus.

Lucas, David (2011). *Lost in the Toy Museum: An Adventure*. London: Walker Books.

McCaughrean, Geraldine (1982). *One Thousand and One Arabian Nights*. Oxford: Oxford University Press.

McCaughrean, Geraldine (2003). *Perseus*. Oxford: Oxford University Press.

MacDonald, George (2015 [1905]). *At the Back of the North Wind*. New York: Mythic Press.

McKay, Hilary (2017a). *Fairy Tales*. London: Macmillan.

McKay, Hilary (2017b). 'Over the Hills and Far Away, or Red Riding Hood and the Piper's Son', in *Fairy Tales*. London: Macmillan.

Macmillan, Angela (ed.) (2012). *A Little, Aloud, for Children*. Oxford: Random House.

Magnason, Andri Snær (2012). *The Story of the Blue Planet*, tr. Julian Meldon D'Arcy, ill. Áslaug Jónsdóttir. New York: Seven Stories Press.

Manning, Mick and Granström, Brita (1997). *What's Under the Bed? A Book About the Earth Beneath Us*. London: Watts.

Mark, Jan (1980). *Nothing to Be Afraid Of*. London: Puffin.

Melville, Herman (1992 [1851]). *Moby Dick*. Ware: Wordsworth Classics.

Mole, John (2004). 'Variation on an Old Rhyme', in *New and Selected Poems*. Calstock: Peterloo Poets.

Monro, Harold (1933a [1915]). 'Milk for the Cat', in *Collected Poems of Harold Monro*. London: Gerald Duckworth.

Monro, Harold (1933b [1915]). 'Overheard on a Saltmarsh', in *Collected Poems of Harold Monro*. London: Gerald Duckworth.

Moore, Lilian (1967). 'If You Catch a Firefly', in *I Feel the Same Way*. New York: Atheneum.

Morpurgo, Michael (2010). *Hansel and Gretel*, ill. Emma Chichester Clark. London: Walker Books.

Moses, Brian (2016a). 'A Cat Called Elvis', in *The Very Best of Brian Moses*. London: Macmillan.

Moses, Brian (2016b). 'Empty Places', in *The Very Best of Brian Moses*. London: Macmillan.

Moses, Brian (2016c). 'December Moon', in *Lost Magic*. London: Macmillan.

Naidoo, Beverley (2018). *Cinderella of the Nile*, ill. Marjan Vafaeian. London: Tiny Owl.

Nesbit, Edith (1993 [1899]). 'The Island of the Nine Whirlpools', in Jan Mark (ed.), *Oxford Book of Children's Stories*. Oxford: Oxford University Press.

Nesbit, Edith (1995 [1904]). *The Phoenix and the Carpet*. London: Puffin Classics.

Nesbit, Edith (1995 [2006]). *The Railway Children*. London: Penguin Popular Classics.

Nesbit, Edith (2002 [1899]). *Five Children and It*. Ware: Wordsworth Editions.

Nesbit, Edith (2018 [1890]). 'Child's Song in Spring', in Susannah Herbert (ed.), *Poetry for a Change*. Hereford: Otter-Barry Books.

Nicholls, Judith (1992). 'Bluebottle', in *Storm's Eye*. Oxford: Oxford University Press.

Nicholls, Judith (2001 [1988]). 'Brian's Picnic', in Roger McGough (ed.), *100 Best Poems for Children*. London: Puffin.

Nicholls, Judith (2009). 'Cockroach', in James Carter and Graham Denton (eds), *Wild! Rhymes That Roar*. London: Macmillan.

Nichols, Grace (1991). 'Don't Cry Caterpillar', in John Agard and Grace Nichols, *No Hickory, No Dickory, No Dock*. London: Puffin.

Nichols, Grace (2009 [1996]). 'Sea-Rock', in Michael Rosen (ed.), *A–Z: The Best Children's Poetry from Agard to Zephaniah*. London: Penguin.

Nova, Karl (2017). 'New Year', in *Rhythm and Poetry*. Steeton: Caboodle Books.

Pinfold, Levi (2016). *Greenling*. London: Bonnier.

Poe, Edgar Allen (1993 [1841]). 'A Descent into the Maelström', in *Tales of Mystery and Imagination*. Ware: Wordsworth Editions.

Proust, Marcel (2003 [1913–1927]). *In Search of Lost Time* [À la recherche du temps perdu], 7 vols. London: Penguin.

Pullman, Philip (2004). *I Was a Rat! Or, The Scarlet Slippers*. London: Random House.

Pullman, Philip (2013). *Grimm Tales for Young and Old*. London: Penguin.

Ransome, Arthur (1916a). 'Daughter of the Snow', in *Old Peter's Russian Tales*. London: Jane Nissen.

Ransome, Arthur (1916b). 'Frost', in *Old Peter's Russian Tales*. London: Jane Nissen.

Ransome, Arthur (1916c). *Old Peter's Russian Tales*. London: Jane Nissen.

Reeves, James (ed.) (1962). *Georgian Poetry*. Harmondsworth: Penguin.

Reeves, James (2009a [1950]). 'The Sea', in *Complete Poems for Children*. London: Faber & Faber.

Reeves, James (2009b [1950]). 'Slowly', in *Complete Poems for Children*. London: Faber & Faber.

Reeves, James (2009c [1955]). 'The Statue', in *Complete Poems for Children*. London: Faber & Faber.

Reeves, James (2009d [1950]). 'The Wind', in *Complete Poems for Children*. London: Faber & Faber.

Rosen, Michael (1981). 'Busy Day', in Roger McGough and Michael Rosen, *You Tell Me*. London: Puffin.

Rosen, Michael (2006). 'Grumble Belly', in *Mustard, Custard, Grumble Belly and Gravy*. London: Bloomsbury.

Rosen, Michael (2015). 'Go-Kart', in *Quick, Let's Get Out of Here*. London: Puffin.

Rossetti, Christina (1947 [1872]). 'What is Pink?', in Jane Werner Watson (ed.), *The Golden Book of Poetry*, ill. Gertrude Espenscheid. New York: Simon & Schuster.

Rossetti, Christina (1979 [1872]). 'Caterpillar', in *Complete Poems of Christina Rossetti*. London: Penguin.

Rossetti, Christina (2003 [1872]). 'The Wind', in *Sing-Song: A Nursery Rhyme Book*. New York: Dover.

Rossetti, Christina (2012 [1904]). 'January Cold Desolate', in Carol Ann Duffy (ed.), *101 Poems for Children: A Laureate's Choice*. London: Macmillan.

Rossetti, Christina (2012 [1872]). 'Hurt No Living Thing', in Carol Ann Duffy (ed.), *101 Poems for Children: A Laureate's Choice*. London: Macmillan.

Rowling, Joanne K. (1997–2007). 'Harry Potter' Series. London: Bloomsbury.

Said, S. F. (2004). *Varjak Paw*, ill. Dave McKean. London: Random House.

Salkey, Andrew (1988). 'Anancy', in Grace Nichols (ed.), *Poetry Jump-Up: A Collection of Black Poetry*. London: Puffin.

Sinclair, Catherine (1993 [1839]). 'Uncle David's Nonsensical Story About Giants and Fairies', in Jan Mark (ed.), *The Oxford Book of Children's Stories*. Oxford: Oxford University Press.

Smart, Christopher (1970 [1762]). 'For I Will Consider My Cat Jeoffry', in *Jubilate Agno*. London: Greenwood Press.

Smith, Stevie (2012). 'The Forlorn Sea', in Carol Ann Duffy (ed.), *101 Poems for Children: A Laureate's Choice*. London: Macmillan.

Socha, Piotr and Grajkowski, Wojciech (2016). *The Book of Bees*. London: Thames & Hudson.

Soundar, Chitra (2016). *Pattan's Pumpkin*, ill. Frane Lessac. Hereford: Otter-Barry Books.

Soundar, Chitra (2018). *You're Safe With Me*, ill. Poonam Mistry. London: Lantana.

Spyri, Johanna (2014 [1881]). *Heidi*. New York: Puffin.

Stevenson, Robert Louis (2008 [1885]). 'My Shadow', in *A Child's Garden of Verses*. London: Puffin.

Summerfield, Geoffrey (ed.) (1970). *Voices: An Anthology of Poetry and Pictures*, 2 vols. (Harmondsworth: Penguin).

Tahvili, Nazli (2018). *Chalk Eagle*. London: Tiny Owl.

Tan, Amy (1989). *The Joy Luck Club*. New York: G. P. Putnam's Sons.

Thomas, Edward (1994 [1915]). 'Words', in *The Works of Edward Thomas*. Ware: Wordsworth Editions.

Thomas, Isabel (2018). *Moth: An Evolution Story*, ill. Daniel Egnéus. London: Bloomsbury.

Thompson, Colin (1995). *How to Live Forever*. Sydney, NSW: Random House.

Turnbull, Ann (1989). *The Sand Horse*. London: Andersen Press.

Villa, Alvaro F. (2014). *Flood*. London: Curious Fox.

Wakeling, Kate (2016a). *Moon Juice: Poems for Children*. Birmingham: Emma Press.

Wakeling, Kate (2016b). 'New Moon', in *Moon Juice: Poems for Children*. Birmingham: Emma Press.

Ward, Helen and Anderson, Wayne (2001). *The Tin Forest*. London: Templar.

Wiesner, David (1988). *Free Fall*. Toronto, ON: HarperCollins.

Wiesner, David (2013). *Mr Wuffles!*. New York: Clarion Books.

Wiesner, David (2017). *Hurricane*. London: Anderson Press.

Wells, Herbert George (2005 [1895]). *The Time Machine*. London: Penguin Classics.

Wells, Herbert George (2017 [1904]). *The Food of the Gods and How It Came to Earth*. Ware: Wordsworth Classics.

Wolfe, Humbert (2012 [1925]). 'Green Candles', in Carol Ann Duffy (ed.), *101 Poems for Children: A Laureate's Choice*. London: Macmillan.

Wordsworth, William (1963 [1804]). 'The Kitten and Falling Leaves', in Edward Blishen (ed.), *Oxford Book of Poetry for Children*. London: Oxford University Press.

Young, Rebecca (2016). *Teacup*, ill. Matt Ottley. New York: Random House.

Zephaniah, Benjamin (2000). 'Who Are We?', in *Wicked World!* London: Puffin.

Secondary sources

Alexander, Robin (2008). *Towards Dialogic Teaching: Rethinking Classroom Talk*, 4th edn. Cambridge: Dialogos.

Beck, Isabel, McKeown, Margaret and Kucan, Linda (2013). *Bringing Words to Life*, 2nd edn. New York: Guilford Press.

Biggs, John B. and Collis, Kevin F. (1982). *Evaluating the Quality of Learning: The SOLO Taxonomy.* New York: Academic Press.

Chambers, Aidan (1991). *Tell Me*. Stroud: Thimble Press.

Claxton, Guy (2005). *Building Learning Power: Helping Young People Become Better Learners*. Bristol: TLO Ltd.

Clements, James (2018). *Teaching English by the Book: Putting Literature at the Heart of the Primary Curriculum*. Abingdon and New York: Routledge.

Cox, Bob (2014). *Opening Doors to Famous Poetry and Prose: Ideas and Resources for Accessing Literary Heritage Works*. Carmarthen: Crown House Publishing.

Cox, Bob (2016a). *Opening Doors to Quality Writing: Ideas for Writing Inspired by Great Writers for Ages 6 to 9*. Carmarthen: Crown House Publishing.

Cox, Bob (2016b). *Opening Doors to Quality Writing: Ideas for Writing Inspired by Great Writers for Ages 10 to 13*. Carmarthen: Crown House Publishing.

Eaglestone, Robert (2019). *Literature: Why It Matters*. Cambridge: Polity Press.

Education Endowment Foundation (2017). *Dialogic Teaching: Evaluation Report and Executive Summary* (July). Available at: https://educationendowmentfoundation. org.uk/public/files/Projects/ Evaluation_Reports/Dialogic_Teaching_ Evaluation_Report.pdf.

Eyre, Deborah (2016). *High Performance Learning: How to Become a World Class School*. Abingdon and New York: Routledge.

Gadsby, Claire (2012). *Perfect Assessment for Learning*. Carmarthen: Independent Thinking Press.

Guppy, Peter and Hughes, Margaret (1999). *The Development of Independent Reading: Reading Support Explained*. Milton Keynes: Open University Press.

Lemov, Doug, Driggs, Colleen and Woolway, Erica (2016). *Reading Reconsidered: A Practical Guide to Rigorous Literacy Instruction*. San Francisco, CA: Jossey-Bass.

Myatt, Mary (2018). *The Curriculum: Gallimaufry to Coherence*. Woodbridge: John Catt Educational.

Oakhill, Jane, Cain, Kate and Elbro, Carsten (2015). *Understanding and Teaching Reading Comprehension: A Handbook*. Abingdon and New York: Routledge.

Quigley, Alex (2018). *Closing the Vocabulary Gap*. Abingdon and New York: Routledge.

Roche, Mary (2014). *Developing Children's Critical Thinking Through Picturebooks*. Abingdon and New York: Routledge.

Sealy, Clare (2017). 'Infernal Inference', *Primary Timery* [blog] (1 May). Available at: https://primarytimery.com/2017/05/01/ infernal-inference/.

Shanahan, Timothy (2017). 'The Instructional Level Concept Revisited: Teaching with Complex Text', *Shanahan on Literacy* [blog] (7 February). Available at: https://shanahanonliteracy.com/blog/

the-instructional-level-concept-revisited-teaching-with-complex-text.

Tannenbaum, Kendra, Torgesen, Joseph and Wagner, Richard (2006). 'Relationships Between Word Knowledge and Reading Comprehension in Third Grade Children', *Scientific Studies of Reading*, 10(4): 381–398.

Tennent, Wayne (2015). *Understanding Reading Comprehension: Processes and Practices*. London: SAGE.

Tennent, Wayne, Reedy, David, Hobsbaum, Angela and Gamble, Nikki (2016). *Guiding Readers – Layers of Meaning: A Handbook for Teaching Reading Comprehension to 7–11 Year Olds*. London: University College London Institute of Education Press.

Tharby, Andy (2017). *Making Every English Lesson Count: Six Principles to Support Great Reading and Writing*. Carmarthen: Crown House Publishing.

Willingham, Daniel T. (2004). 'Ask the Cognitive Scientist: Practice Makes Perfect – But Only If You Practice Beyond the Point of Perfection', *American Educator* (spring). Available at: https://www.aft.org/periodical/american-educator/spring-2004/ask-cognitive-scientist.

Useful websites

Book Trust: www.booktrust.org.uk

Centre for Literacy in Primary Education: www.clpe.org.uk

Changing Minds (Socratic questions): http://changingminds.org/techniques/questioning/socratic_questions.htm

Education Endowment Foundation: https://educationendowmentfoundation.org.uk

English and Media Centre: www.englishandmedia.co.uk

English Association (4–11 online articles): www2.le.ac.uk/offices/english-association/primary/primary-plus/411online

High Performance Learning: www.highperformancelearning.co.uk

Into Film: www.intofilm.org

Just Imagine Story Centre: www.justimagine.co.uk

Let's Think – Cognitive Acceleration: www.letsthink.org.uk

Let's Think in English: www.letsthinkinenglish.org

Michael Rosen: www.michaelrosen.co.uk

More Able and Talented (Wales): http://matwales.org

National Association for the Teaching of English: www.nate.org.uk

National Literacy Trust: www.literacytrust.org.uk

National Poetry Day: www.nationalpoetryday.co.uk

Poetry Archive: www.poetryarchive.org

Poetry by Heart: www.poetrybyheart.org.uk

Poetry Society: www.poetrysociety.org.uk

Potential Plus UK: www.potentialplusuk.org

Society for the Advancement of Philosophical Enquiry and Reflection in Education: www.sapere.org.uk

SOLO taxonomy: www.johnbiggs.com.au/academic/solo-taxonomy

Talk for Writing: www.talk4writing.co.uk

United Kingdom Literacy Association: https://ukla.org

Writing for Pleasure Centre: www.writing4pleasure.com

List of Downloadable Resources

Available from: https://crownhouse.co.uk/ featured/opening-doors-richer-6-9

About the Authors

Bob Cox

Having taught English for twenty-three years, Bob Cox is now an independent education consultant, writer and teacher coach who works nationally and internationally to support outstanding learning. Bob also delivers keynotes for national associations, multi-academy trusts and local authorities, as more schools integrate 'Opening Doors' strategies into their curriculum design.

Leah Crawford

Leah Crawford has fifteen years' experience as a local authority English inspector and adviser, working across both the primary and secondary phases, and now leads the Thinktalk education consultancy. She is an associate tutor on King's College London's Let's Think in English cognitive acceleration programme and also works in support of a European Erasmus project on the assessment of thinking skills.

Verity Jones

Having spent over a decade working in education – as a teacher, a deputy head and an adviser – Verity Jones is now a senior lecturer at the University of the West of England, Bristol. She continues to provide training for both new and experienced teachers on how to ensure every child reaches their potential.